# onions

**onions**  ● Rosemary Moon

onions

**APPLE**

A QUINTET BOOK

Published by The Apple Press
6 Blundell Street
London N7 9BH

ISBN 1-84092-177-3

This book was designed and produced by
Quintet Publishing Limited
6 Blundell Street
London N7 9BH

Creative Director: Richard Dewing
Art Director: Paula Marchant
Design: Paul Wright
Project Editor: Debbie Foy
Editor: Anna Bennett

Typeset in Great Britain by
Central Southern Typesetters, Eastbourne
Manufactured in Malaysia by CH Color Scan Sdn. Bhd.
Printed in China by Leefung-Asco Printers Ltd.

Picture Credits
Seaspring Photos: p8, 19, 20, 21; ET Archive: p10, p11, p12; Life File: p5, p14

*This book is for Tony, who loves onions, and for Pat,
for all the tears and especially the happy ones.*

# Contents

# Acknowledgements

There are many people who should be thanked for their roles in the production of the book. My husband Nick is always enthusiastic about my food and, bless him, even seems to cope when there is the occasional need to eat onions for breakfast! The herring and onion salad went down a treat at 7.30 am! Toby Moon, our much-loved gourmand Shetland Sheepdog, was less enthusiastic about this project than some (a book on cheese would be his idea of heaven), but he was introduced to herring roe for breakfast through that very same salad and – I can tell you – herring roe is one of the things that Shelties like best.

So often a cookbook is judged on its photographs and those in this volume are truly mouthwatering. So special thanks are due to Tim Ferguson-Hill, the photographer, and to Emma Patmore, the home economist and food stylist. I know what long days the team worked and I am delighted with the results – thank you both.

My great thanks are due to my horticultural friends at West Dean Gardens near Chichester in Sussex. Sarah Wain explained all sorts of matters horticultural in her patient Melbourne manner, and Stuart the Champion Onion Man might have gossiped away rather too many of his top tips for prize-winning onions. Their time was generously given and much appreciated.

We have a marvellous bunch of friends who are always happy to munch their way through recipe tests, kindly commenting and suggesting the occasional tweak. Those who have done sterling eating work on this project include: Mum and Dad Noble who tackled some of the richer dishes with relish and pronounced them delicious; Jimbo and Sarah from West Dean; Sue from down the road; James and Sarah; and Dawn and Martin over the road, who are quite new in the village and think recipe testing is an excellent idea. And to everyone else who has gathered round the dining table – thank you all.

*Rosemary Moon.*

# about the onion

*Many pieces of silver were spent on the purchase of onions to feed the labourers building the Great Pyramids of Egypt. Without onions, the Seven Wonders of the World might only have been six. This chapter details the global history of the onion, as well as exploring the many varieties available to the home cook.*

Chives, with their purple flower heads almost ready to burst open, make a decorative and unusual edging to flower and vegetable borders.

# introduction

The onion is one of the oldest vegetables known to man and an essential ingredient in just about every cuisine of the world. It is hard to imagine a vegetable basket without onions for they are the basis of so many different recipes.

Onions are edible alliums, or lilies. Many varieties exist, all of which are edible, but only a certain number are commonly used for culinary purposes, because some of the more decorative varieties are bitter-tasting and, although not actually poisonous, are simply not palatable. Today, as more and more people look for natural healing remedies, onions are also keenly popular for their medicinal properties. Alliums are also very beautiful in the garden, where their decorative heads form a spectacular display. I always leave one or two leeks and onions to go to seed, giving me a display of large purple flower heads.

This book explores the versatility of the onion. When I was asked to write it I thought it sounded like a pretty straightforward general cookbook. However, a week or so into the recipe testing and I was amazed at just

how easy it is to make the onion the star of the dish! Not just by upping the quantities so that it dominates, but by cooking the onions slowly to draw out the delicious sweetness that is onions, a flavour unknown to anyone who simply fries them quickly at the beginning of a dish before adding other ingredients.

Raw, sliced, sautéed, chopped, stewed, pickled, roasted or baked – however an onion is cooked it is a delight and an essential, not only for infinitely variable international cuisine, but also for a healthy and flavoursome diet. And what of the occasional tears? Well, that's a small price to pay. Experiment and enjoy!

The scent of wild garlic often greets you long before the plants, with their delicate white flowers, come into view.

# The onion *in history*

Onions and their relatives have been grown since humans started to cultivate the land. They were an essential part of the diet of the slaves who built the Great Pyramids in Egypt. One of the pyramids built in 2500 BC includes an inscription revealing that onions, garlic and radishes had been purchased with silver to feed the workers. Although this was a great expense, it was deemed necessary both to keep the workforce healthy and to keep them motivated and working well. Onions of various forms are also depicted in murals in Egyptian and other ancient tombs. Some of the colour washes for these paintings would have been made from steeped onion skins, just as the colour was used to dye cloth until comparatively recent times.

The Bible is full of references to onions. One of the earliest is the Israelites bemoaning their poor diet after they fled from Egypt, citing the fish which they had enjoyed with cucumbers and onions, among other vegetables. Almost two thousand years later, at the time of the Roman Empire, historians were writing of onions as essential vegetables to be grown in market gardens to supply the townspeople. By this time, the first century AD, onions were grown widely throughout the known world – the Roman Empire and Asia, including China—but they were unknown, even in any wild form, in the Americas and Australia. Whether the Romans actually introduced them throughout Europe I do not know, but they did take a great number of their foods with them as they expanded the Roman Empire northwards, so they may well have introduced garlic even if onions were already flourishing.

Foods enjoy heights and depths of popularity and fashion. Garlic chives, for example, are a mildly garlic-flavoured variety of chive, most certainly a member of the onion family. A relatively new introduction to my herb garden, these aromatic leaves, also called Chinese chives, are known to have existed in China from at least 500 BC, when they were offered in sacrifice with lamb. They soon featured in Japanese culinary records as well, but it seems to have been many years before they reached the West.

Although many members of the onion family are known to exist in the wild – elephant garlic often grows freely near the sites of early Christian monasteries, possibly having self-perpetuated after a period of cultivation by the monks, and leeks were still found in the wild quite recently, especially in Ireland – onions themselves are now only cultivated. Like wheat and many other essential basic commodities, it is thought that onions originated in the area to the west and north of India and spread through cultivation to all other parts of the temperate and subtropical world with the early explorers and settlers. This is how many crops were established, although varieties that grew well in one place were not always a success in another area.

## Onions reach the New Worlds

Christopher Columbus is credited with introducing onions to the Americas at the end of the fifteenth century. Legend has it that the name Chicago is a derivation of a Native American word meaning rotting or smelly onions and Chicago has certainly always been a major onion-growing area.

Onions were introduced to Australia by the first English settlers in 1787. They took onion seeds and sets (small bulbs grown from seed the previous season) with them, regarding them as culinary essentials. By the end of the eighteenth century this most versatile of vegetables was known worldwide. Much work was still to be done, however, in producing the correct cultivars for growing in such an enormous variety of climatic conditions.

*The Emperor Nero. Onions were an essential crop in Rome for feeding the townspeople and were grown extensively in market gardens.*

*Onions played an important role in the legendary Roman banquets, depicted in this second-century AD pavement mosaic.*

# The onion *family*

The onion family also includes garlic, leeks and chives but this book focuses primarily on the onion and its many uses in cooking, both as a central and supporting ingredient. Here, however, is a brief introduction to the onion's relatives:

**Chives** are a must in any herb garden, and are usually grown there rather than in the main vegetable beds as they are ideally suited to alpine slopes and rocky crevices. Only the leaves and flowers are eaten, not the bulb. The leaves, delicately onion-flavoured, should be snipped with scissors. Leave chives to self-seed in cracks on your garden steps: their little purple flower heads are attractive to look at and also taste good in salads. Chives are more widely grown than any other type of edible allium as they can withstand most climatic conditions. The name chive derives from the Latin *cepa* and was originally used to describe any small plant of the onion family. **Garlic chives** are used in the same way as common chives, although they are stronger in flavour. Known since ancient times in China, where this plant originates, these chives add a very special flavour to salads. Garlic chives are larger than the common chive and they make impressive edging plants.

**Garlic** is almost a cult vegetable and is, in my opinion, much maligned through over-use. Like a glimpse of stocking, it should be much more of a suggestion than a blatant flavour statement. Used too heavily it can be

unpleasant but added subtly to a dish it can introduce an interesting flavour. A cut clove rubbed around a salad bowl or over toasted bread is heavenly.

**Onion Weed** and **Ramsons** are easy to confuse. The flower stems of the former are triangular in shape and have a white flower. Onion weed naturalizes quickly and invasively and is as likely to be found on a wooded foreshore as it is by streams and in other damp, shady places. Ramsons is the traditional name for wild garlic and is native to the UK and northern Europe. Although ramsons usually grows by streams and in wooded areas, the fashionable area of Ramsons Dock in south London would suggest that the plant might once have been found in abundance along the banks of the River Thames. Confusion between ramsons and onion weed occurs as both plants have a similar habitat and white flowers – the stem is the most helpful identification pointer for non-botanists.

**Welsh Onions** are more commonly, if incorrectly, known as **Spring Onions, Green Onions,** or **Scallions.** The confusion arises as spring onion is not a true term, but is often used for Welsh onions, the species *Alluim fistulosum*, which are harvested early when small and are thought to have been introduced into northern Europe through Russia from China. It is possible that the term derives from the Anglo-Saxon *waelise* or the German *welsch*, meaning foreign. They are the best salad onions and are commonly used raw, although many people prefer to cook them lightly, especially in stir-fries.

**Leeks** are a great vegetable for gardeners and cooks alike. They are as versatile as onions, survive well in the garden throughout a temperate winter and grow tall, erect and branching, providing almost architectural plants in the flower borders. As ancient as onions, leeks were certainly spread throughout Europe by the Romans who were very partial to this vegetable. It is said that the Emperor Nero ate leeks to improve his singing voice. The leek is the national emblem of Wales, and is popularly thought to have become so as Welsh soldiers wore a leek pinned to their clothes as a mark of identification, so that they did not kill each other in battle. It is interesting to note that the Welsh name for daffodils, the other national mascot, is *Cenin Pedr*, or St. Peter's Leek.

**Shallots** are less widely grown by amateur gardeners than onions, and yet they provide good results and yield from a small area. They are also part of a great gardening heritage and store well throughout the winter. Shallots are valuable to cooks as they provide a great deal of flavour from very little bulk – they are ideal for sauces and for incorporating into pastry and dough. In the garden they

**Welsh**

**Shallots**

**Mild**

**Pickling**

**Spanish**

**White**

**Red**

**Oso**

**Standard**

are also a useful border plant and may help to protect the vegetable garden from rabbits, who are deterred by their smell. Shallots may be red, golden, round or elongated. The fashionable banana shallot, popular with chefs because it is twice the size of a regular bulb, used to be known as the chicken's thigh shallot, which aptly describes its shape.

Yellow onions are the most common onion. They are the general-purpose workhorses of the onion family and are seldom sold by variety as the best onions for the time of year will be offered for sale, home produced or imported. Spanish and Sweet Bermuda onions are large, well-flavoured onions, but they are not as pungent as the majority of yellow onions. They can be eaten raw (they are best very thinly sliced for this) and are either yellow or white. The Bermuda has slightly flattened ends. Pearl or Silverskin onions are a bulb about 2.5 cm (1 in) in diameter. They have papery outer skins and are usually used whole. Red onions originated in Italy and are mainly eaten raw. They have a strong but mild flavour. Sweet onions such as Vidalia, Oso and Walla Walla are truly sweet and make very interesting pies and tarts. They are also excellent roasted, then used in a salad. Most sweet onions are white but the American Walla Walla, the sweetest of them all, is yellow.

Onion Sprouts are occasionally found commercially grown. Onion seeds from health food shops, which have not been treated with fungicide, should sprout at home in much the same way as bean sprouts. Place the seeds on several layers of kitchen paper in a plastic tray pierced all over the base with holes. Carefully soak the tray through with cold water twice a day and keep in a warm, dark place. Once beginning to sprout, place the tray on a bright windowsill until the sprouts are about 2.5 cm (1 in ) long. Eat in salads, or use as a garnish for lightly spiced foods. Onion sprouts are also delicious in cream cheese sandwiches.

The Tree Onion, or Egyptian Onion, is grown mainly as a decorative garden plant rather than as a culinary crop, although it is edible. The onions, or bulbils, are held proudly aloft on thick onion stems, usually 60 cm (2 ft) from the ground. They are a good topic of conversation when showing friends around the garden, and I have grown them in both vegetable and flower borders.

*A selection of onions and shallots at Le Lavandou market, on the Côte d'Azur, France.*

*Cordoba, one of the gastronomic centres of Spain. Spanish onions are usually large and mild, yet distinctive in flavour.*

## *The global* onion

Onions are grown and used so widely throughout the world that I cannot think of a single cuisine that does not use them – indeed, that does not rely heavily upon them.

Whether chopped or sliced and cooked as the basis of a casserole, stew or sauce, sliced and served as a salad or a garnish or prepared as a pickle you will find onions as a major ingredient in dishes in every cuisine, from haggis in Scotland, through the pizzas of Italy and the curries of India to the funky hot salad infusions of the Pacific Rim.

Very few countries are self-sufficient in onions as stocks are nearly always imported to complement the home-growing season, but yellow, Spanish and red onions, along with shallots and spring onions are available in most countries year round. Sweet onions, which are more restricted in their area of growth (mostly the United States), are generally only available in the winter months, and pickling onions are also seasonal.

Onions can be used as a basic ingredient; providing texture by being added as a crunchy garnish; or to add flavour to what would otherwise be a very bland dish. Much Scottish and Irish cookery, which traditionally relies mainly on oats, benefits greatly from the addition of onion

– an oatmeal soup or stuffing would be little more than a thickened gruel without an onion, and fish soups made with potatoes and smoked fish might also be bland and dull but for the inclusion of onion which turns them into a culinary delight, albeit simple and direct.

French cuisine remains one of the greatest in the world, and its rich stews and casseroles achieve an amazing depth of flavour when the onions are cooked slowly in olive oil while the meat and other ingredients are prepared for the pot. Indeed, the French *Pissaladière* (page 128), a pizza-like dish of bread dough topped with stewed onions, thyme, olives and anchovies, is, I think, one of the richest and most delicious onion dishes in the world. The restorative properties of French Onion Soup (page 36) consumed as a pick-me-up after a night on the town more than illustrate the versatility of the onion and its rich, thick flavours.

A good Greek salad is hard to imagine without slices of raw onion, often red and slightly sweet yet pungent, to offset the richness of the cheese, olives and olive oil. Can a tomato salad function without onions, whether prepared in the Mediterranean, or in India to accompany crispy poppadoms or rich, thick curries? Indeed, once you start experimenting with Indian sauces you begin to explore another facet of onion cookery: their use as the basis of a

CALLEJON DE URIZAR

*Onions and other local vegetables displayed in the shade outside a village shop in Spain.*

thick puréed sauce which releases and uses the water in the onions, rather than vast quantities of additional liquids. Such curry pastes and blends are also used in any cuisine where spices are introduced in thickened sauces. Garlic and ginger are often blended with the onions, and the mixture is then fried with spices as the base of the dish. Sometimes these pastes are thickened with nuts, usually almonds or macadamias, and I often reach for the poppy seeds as well, to add extra crunch to the sauce. Another way to add crispness is to garnish a dish with spring onions.

Spring onions are also widely used in Chinese cookery, and generous chunks of onions are often braised along with peppers, aubergines and Chinese leaves in traditional vegetarian dishes. Chinese cookery without onions is especially unthinkable, as the vegetables add crunch and flavour to many classic dishes.

In North America and Australia, the real homes of fusion cookery, the bright vibrant flavours of modern cuisine rely on onions just as much as the more traditional dishes of the many, many cultures which now add their culinary heritage to the melting pot which is modern cuisine. Salsas, chili and onion pastes and jams and fried onions with burgers have just as much to add to the

culinary scene as the sweet onions beloved of the Americans and the spices of the South.

As essential ingredients, both onions and shallots have their place in the culinary heritage of the world. In terms of nutritive value, onions are quite good sources of vitamins A and C, and the B Group vitamins niacin, riboflavin and thiamine. Made up of about 90 per cent water, they are very low in calories, although frying them will of course alter that. Their 1.4 per cent protein content is reasonable for a vegetable, and carbohydrates present include glucose, fructose and sucrose.

All sorts of extraordinary medicinal claims have been made about onions throughout history, ranging from improving failing eyesight to reducing blood pressure, acting as a laxative, improving circulation and increasing lust. An early recipe to prevent hair loss called for a mixture of onion juice and honey to be rubbed into the scalp twice daily, while the juice when combined with vinegar was used to treat pimples.

Eating onions has always been regarded as a good natural remedy for the common cold, although in olden times slices of raw onion simply placed inside your shoe were believed to relieve the symptoms. Undoubtedly, they help to relieve congestion, but I am sure most of us would balk at sniffing the juice, which is claimed to clear your head. In Trinidad, water in which onions have been boiled is used to treat coughs and colds. Onions are also said to counteract chest infections.

Onions, and other members of the allium family, are both antiseptic and antibiotic. Medical research, conducted as a follow-up to the 1993 paper 'Garlic's Potential Role in Reducing Heart Disease', published in the *British Journal of Clinical Practice*, has shown that garlic can help to reduce the build-up of cholesterol on artery walls.

If you are bitten by an insect, tear the tops off some spring onions, crush them and rub on to the affected area. The juice of the onions will take away some of the sting and help to relieve the itching. Some people recommend raw onion for bee stings.

# Why do onions *make you cry?*

There is no mystery to this. Onions contain a water-soluble organic sulphur compound called alliin, referred to in onions as the lacrimatory precursor – the harbinger of tears. This is present in varying amounts in different onions, hence some varieties will reduce you to tears more readily than others. When the onion bulb is cut the enzyme alliinase acts on the alliin to produce an organic sulphur compound which reacts with water (the moisture in your eyes as you are standing over the onion with your knife) to produce sulphuric acid. It is the acid which produces tears and makes your eyes sting.

*Slicing an onion right through, keeping its root intact, helps to prevent tears when chopping or slicing.*

## *Peeling without* tears

Small pickling onions and shallots take a good deal of time to prepare and can result in a great deal of discomfort. When you cut off the root, which loosens the skins, you also release the onion juices, along with your tears. The best way to peel these small onions is to pour boiling water over them and leave them to soak for 5 minutes – the skins should then slip off easily. I usually cut away the top of the onion then peel the papery outer layers away towards the root. Leaving the root intact while chopping or slicing helps enormously. Much research has been done, especially by Eric Block in 'The Chemistry of Garlic and Onions', published by *Scientific American*, which has proved that chilling onions before you chop them reduces the lacrimatory factor and thus stops tears, but do wrap them well before placing them in the fridge or their smell will taint everything else. Peeling under running water also helps by washing the water-soluble factor away.

*All the hard work done – peeled shallots, ready for cooking or pickling.*

# Growing *onions*

It is unlikely that the first shipment of onion seeds taken from England to Australia could have been successful because onion cultivars have to be carefully matched to their growing conditions. Those that grow well in North America, Europe and Asia are known as long-day cultivars, whereas short-day cultivars are required for most of Australia, southernmost areas requiring intermediate-day cultivars. Most onions like to grow in temperatures of between 20 and 25°C (68 and 77°F). If it is too cold the bulbs will not form; too hot and the bulbs will be stunted in growth.

## *Onion* shapes

Onions and shallots are either torpedo-shaped, flat or globular. Flat onions ripen more quickly and will therefore generally store better. If you are trying to grow for the whole season, you should mix your varieties to accommodate ripening and storage. When selecting onions and shallots to grow, you should seek out your local horticultural society and speak to some of the members to find out which varieties suit the local soil and climate.

The basic difference between onions and shallots, apart from size, is that onions are single bulbs, whereas shallots grow in clusters which develop from a single bulb. Thus shallots are grown from bulbs but onions may be grown either from seed or sets – sets are small bulbs from the previous season which will mature more quickly than onions from seed, an important consideration in the more northerly growing areas. They are also less likely to be attacked by onion fly, one of the onion grower's most hated enemies. Shallots are traditionally planted on the shortest day of the year and harvested on the longest, although only a few varieties are actually recommended for such traditional growing. The more bolt-resistant varieties such as Sante and Topper should not be sown until early spring, although Golden Gourmet, which produces a fine clump of flavoursome shallots, may be sown earlier. For those wanting a red shallot, try Success, which produces mild but tasty bulbs, or Springfield, a new variety with a strongly flavoured, pinkish flesh. Springfield is particularly recommended for pickling. Hative de Niort produces deep, flask-shaped bulbs with a traditional red-brown skin, and cuts into uniform, circular rings.

Shallots and onion sets should be pressed into prepared soil so that just their tops are showing – this is meant to discourage the birds from pulling them all up, but I have found it to be a wise precaution to make a cat's cradle of black cotton thread over the onion bed as protection, but a length of muslin will work equally well.

## *Growing for* greatness

Producing a champion onion is one of the major aims of the amateur horticulturist, although the cook may not be so interested in giant, heavy onions. Most gardeners, including myself, are delighted to get a crop of good size that has ripened and dried before the weather breaks.

Onions require a well-drained, fertile soil which is weed-free at planting time and is kept that way, because the young seedlings are quickly and easily strangled by more vigorous growth. The bulbs are easily damaged, so weed by hand and do not hoe. The onions must be kept evenly watered during the growing period and may be fed with a balanced liquid feed if the spring is cold and they make a slow start. Onions and potatoes are quite often grown together because they require similar conditions.

## *Make the* break

Much of the skill in growing onions comes at the end of the season. The tops wilt when the onions are ready. Some people then fold them over to hasten ripening, but others say that this might damage the plant and shorten the storage life. Once the tops go, carefully insert a fork under the onions and break the contact of the root with the soil. If the weather is dry, leave the onions on the surface of the soil in the sun to dry. This might also be done on wire mesh in an open airy position – don't try to ripen onions in a shed or any other closed space because plenty of circulating air is the secret of successful storage.

*Always use culinary onion seed, sold with other herbs and spices.*

*Onion seedlings soon show through and start to establish themselves.*

*Traditional varieties of shallots, and a few onions, may be planted in the winter for an earlier crop.*

*Bulbing onions ready to begin harvesting.*

*Onions usually produce a lot of tall green growth before the bulbs start to swell.*

*These onions are ready to be 'lifted', before allowing them to dry out thoroughly in the sun.*

# Preserving *and pickling*

The most common way to preserve onions, other than by drying, is by pickling. Small onions are brined and then steeped whole in vinegar to be eaten with salads and sandwiches. It is not known for certain when the tradition of pickling onions began. Pickled onions were certainly often made at home in the mid-eighteenth century but usually as a thrifty way of making use of small bulbs which had not grown to a useful culinary size.

Herbs and spices used in onion pickles are peppercorns, allspice and bay leaves, although coriander seed and dried chillies are also becoming popular for hotter varieties of preserves. Flavour is principally determined by the type of vinegar used – the most common is malt vinegar, a sharp, dark brown by-product of the beer-brewing industry. A lighter cider vinegar may also be used, however, and white wine vinegar has also been favoured by some cooks, notably Eliza Acton. A much-loved, recently discovered deli treat is pickled onions in balsamic vinegar – sweet, nutty and delicious. Much of the flavour of pickled onions also depends on the actual bulb used – I much prefer a mild variety such as Topper or the Paris Silver Skin, but those who like to breathe fire for an hour or so after eating should prepare their pickles with hotter varieties of onion such as Springfield.

Pickles, relishes and chutneys almost inevitably have a high proportion of onions, whatever the other ingredients, and before refrigeration must have provided a welcome burst of flavour during the dull winter months.

*Shallots or baby button onions are best for pickling.*

# Storing *onions*

Like all produce to be kept for later use, onions are best stored in a cool, dark place like a shed or a garage, but it must be frost-free. If onions freeze, their cell structure will rupture on thawing and the crop will be wasted if not used immediately. Bulbs can be stored in loose bunches, or hung in nets if you have no time or inclination to plait them in the traditional way. Do check them regularly and remove any which are soft to avoid spoiling the whole crop. Onions generally keep better when hung, rather than being stored in boxes.

*Onions drying out in the sun. If the soil is wet the onions are best lifted on to a rack.*

# Cooking *with onions*

*Onions are an essential ingredient in chutneys, savoury fruit sauces and salads as well as in casseroles.*

An ingredient as versatile as an onion may be cooked in a number of ways to fulfil its culinary potential.

**Sautéing or Frying** is usually done in oil or butter and is the classic way to begin a large number of recipes. Some call for the onions to be quickly softened to a state of translucency, but you will find that the longer this takes the better (15 to 20 minutes is ideal) because this releases the natural sweetness of the onions.

**Puréeing** is really a preparation rather than a cooking method. Onions are blended to a thick paste to be fried, usually after spices, as the basis of many Indian, Thai and Pacific Rim dishes. The puréed onions form not only the main ingredient but also the thickener for the sauce.

**Baking** may be done in or out of the skins, although the skins will help to hold the onions together during cooking. Most onions to be baked should be par-boiled first.

**Roasting** is a fashionable way of cooking onions (and many root vegetables) at high temperatures in a little olive oil for flavour. Roasting produces a deliciously caramelized outer crust that is sweet to the taste.

**Boiling** is a good way of softening onions which are going to be finished in another way, e.g. in a sauce or topped with breadcrumbs and grilled. Leave small onions whole, or chop large ones into big chunks.

**Braising** in a little stock or gravy produces an almost pot-roast effect.

**Deep-frying** is usually reserved for onion rings, either floured or battered. These are a classic accompaniment to steaks.

# Easy *onion flavours*

There are a number of ways of adding extra onion flavour to dishes without actually using onions. One of the easiest is dried onion soup mix, which is great in breads, scones and mixed into breadcrumbs for crisp toppings. Onion-flavoured salt is good sprinkled over salads – try it also over tomatoes on toast. Onion stock can be bought, but I often make my own, by simmering onion skins in water with a few seasonings, especially if I have been using a lot of onions. This broth is very useful and goes well in almost any dish.

## Complementary foods and flavours

A few basic foods and flavourings are natural partners to onions. One is cheese – try strong yellow onions with a robust Cheddar, or sweet Vidalias with a nutty Swiss cheese such as Emmenthal. Olives and onions go well together, and anchovies are also a very worthy partner. My favourite support herbs for onions are thyme, either common or lemon, and bay leaf. A good spice is mace (the aromatic outer casing of the nutmeg).

*Nutty Swiss Emmenthal cheese is especially good with a sweet white onion such as Vidalia.*

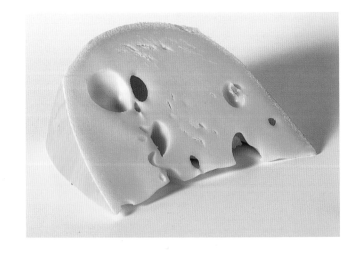

# How to chop *an onion properly*

This is one of the most basic skills to learn in the kitchen. I always try to leave the root intact while chopping, and it is essential to use a very sharp knife, preferably with a large blade, to do this properly.

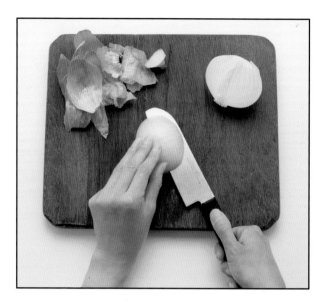

1. Peel off the papery skin, chopping off the top of the onion but leaving the root intact. Cut in half through the onion and the root.

2. Place the onion on a board, cut side down, and slice crossways towards the root, but not right up to it, making three, four or five cuts, depending on the size of the onion.

3. Now cut lengthways, again not right through to the root, three, four or five times.

4. Finally cut crossways again, across the onion, slicing it finely. As you do so, the onion should fall on to the board in neat dice until you reach the root. Chop any flesh left around the root, then discard it.

# What to drink *with onions*

An ingredient of such eclectic usage is difficult to match too specifically to a particular style of wine or beer and it is best to accompany your chosen onion dish with your favorite tipple. Most onion dishes are fairly robust, however, and demand a drink which will not be lost or overwhelmed. My preference in wines is for reds, and most grape varieties will match onion cuisine well. The traditional casseroles and stews of regional France are all served with the local wines, and purists would argue that a Beef Bourguignon should never be drunk with anything other than a Burgundy, although such rigidity is becoming a thing of the past. Choose a full-bodied red such as Cabernet Sauvignon, Merlot or a country red for stews and casseroles, whereas a lighter Gamay, Chinon or Zinfandel will sit well with onion-based vegetarian dishes. That said, a robust and full-bodied red with a touch of challenging roughness, such as a Burgundy, is necessary to stand up to the bold richness of a *Pissaladière* (page 128). White wines should be full-flavoured and the ever-popular Chardonnay, especially if oaked, will complement most onion dishes extremely well, although I would suggest a lighter, crisper Sauvignon blanc with many spicier, lighter dishes and onion-topped salads.

Many rich Belgian and Flemish beers go well with onion-based dishes, whereas English dark beers are great with rich casseroles and pies. Together, beer and onions produce wonderful flavours in slow-cooked dishes and are also natural partners to cheese and onion-flavoured breads, or pies to be served with salads and pickles. Beer, onions and bread are a classic combination as is seen in the popularity of English pub food, especially Ploughman's Lunches (page 130).

*A simple lunch of salad, cheese, bread and onions is best washed down with a glass of beer.*

# sauces, pickles & stuffings

*Onions are the essential ingredient in so many pickles and sauces,
adding relish and flavour to main dishes and entrées. Slow simmered
for depth of flavour, or bound into a forcemeat of crumbs and herbs,
the onion is an excellent supporting ingredient.*

# sweet onion *and apple chutney*

*Makes about 1.8 kg (4 lb)*

1.5 kg (3¼ lb) onions, chopped
1.5 kg (3¼ lb) cooking apples, peeled, cored and diced
700 mL (1¼ pints) sultanas
Grated zest and juice of 2 lemons
750 g (1¾ lb) soft dark brown sugar
600 mL (1 pint) malt vinegar

A mild, fruity chutney containing no spices at all. Try it in cheese sandwiches, with cheese on toast and with meat dishes such as shepherd's pie.

**Preparation time: 30 minutes Cooking time: 1 hour**

Place all the ingredients in a large preserving pan and heat gently until the sugar has dissolved, stirring all the time.

Bring to the boil, and allow to simmer for 30 to 40 minutes or until thickened with all the liquid absorbed.

Meanwhile, scrub preserving jars in hot, soapy water, then rinse thoroughly. Heat jars at 180°C/350°F/Gas Mark 4 for 15 minutes.

Pour chutney mixture into jars immediately, seal and label. This chutney does not need to mature and will keep well for about a year.

# traditional *pickled onions*

*Makes about 2¼ lb (1 kg)*

2¼ lb (1 kg) pickling onions or small shallots
125 mL (4 fl oz) sea salt
1 quart (1L) water
½ cup (125 mL) sugar, preferably unrefined
1L (1¾ pints) malt vinegar
2 Tbsp pickling spice or coriander seeds

I'm sure it's peeling the onions that puts people off pickling their own! Pouring boiling water over the onions and leaving them for 5 minutes prior to peeling can make the skins easier to slip off. I add sugar to my onions because I like them slightly sweet, but it's not essential.

**Preparation time: 20 minutes, plus 2 days for brining**
**Spicing and filling time: 2½ hours for vinegar; 10-15 minutes to fill the jars**

Cut a small slice from each end of the onions, place them in a bowl, and cover with boiling water. Leave for 5 minutes, then drain the onions and run them under cold water until cool enough to handle. Slip off the skins.

Stir the salt into the water until dissolved, then pour the brine over the onions in a mixing bowl. Put a plate on the onions in the bowl, to stop them bobbing up out of the brine. Cover and leave for 48 hours – any less and the onions will be soft; some pickling experts say 3 days, but I find 2 days is right.

Place the sugar, vinegar and spice in a covered pan and bring almost to the boil. Stir to ensure the sugar is dissolved, cover then leave for 2 hours or until the vinegar is cold. Strain to remove the spices.

Drain and thoroughly rinse the onions, then pack them tightly into clean pickle jars – really push them in. Add enough cold vinegar to cover the onions completely.

Seal the jars with screw-top lids, then label. Leave to mature for at least a month before eating.

*sweet onion and apple chutney*

# walnut *and onion chutney*

*Makes about*
*1 Kg (2¼ lb)*

1 kg (2¼ lb) onions, thinly
 sliced
4 Tbsp olive oil
500 g (1 lb 2 oz) apples,
 peeled, cored and chopped
250 mL (9 fl oz) red wine
225 g (8 oz) sugar, preferably
 unrefined
2 tsp coarse sea salt
1 tsp black pepper
100 mL (3½ fl oz) red wine
 vinegar
350 g (12 oz) walnut pieces
Lemon juice to taste

A cross between a traditional chutney and the now-fashionable onion marmalades, the texture of this relish combines the crunch of nuts with a fruity onion base. It should be treated like a marmalade, and kept in the fridge once opened. Eat within 3 to 4 weeks.

**Preparation time: 15 minutes Cooking time: 1¼ hours**

Cook the onions in the oil in a large deep frying pan for 10 minutes until well softened, then add the apples and red wine. Simmer for 20 minutes, until both the onions and apples are well cooked.

Stir in the sugar, salt and pepper and vinegar and cook for a further 30 minutes, until the chutney is thickened and most of the liquid has been absorbed.

Add the walnuts and lemon juice and stir them evenly throughout the mixture. Continue cooking for a further 10 minutes until all the liquid has gone.

Scrub preserving jars in hot, soapy water, then rinse thoroughly. Heat jars at 180°C/350°F/Gas Mark 4 for 15 minutes. Pack chutney mixture into the jars, seal and label.

# onion *sauce*

*Serves 4 to 6*

3 to 4 large onions, cut into
 6 or 8 segments depending
 on size
6 black peppercorns
1 bay leaf
4 Tbsp butter
3 Tbsp plain flour
250 mL (9 fl oz) milk
Salt and black pepper

Another culinary classic, this goes very well with roast lamb. Any leftovers always mix well with cold meat in pilafs or shepherd's pie. I like to leave my onions in large segments, to give the sauce texture. You can use all onion water if you prefer, and add 3–4 tablespoons powdered dried milk to it.

**Preparation time: 15 minutes Cooking time: 10 minutes**

Place the onions in a saucepan with the peppercorns and bay and just enough cold water to cover. Bring to the boil, then cover and simmer for 10 minutes. Drain the onions, reserving the water, and discard the peppercorns and bay leaf.

Heat the butter, flour, milk and 250 mL (9 fl oz) of the onion water together in the pan, stirring all the time. Bring to the boil, then add the drained onions and cook for a further 2 to 3 minutes. Add a little more onion liquor if the sauce is too thick.

Season to taste and serve with roast lamb.

*walnut and onion chutney*

# onion *and olive sauce*

*Serves 4*

3 large onions, finely sliced
4 Tbsp olive oil
Salt and black pepper
3 to 4 large sprigs thyme
Finely grated zest and juice of
  1 lemon
250 mL (9 fl oz) fish or
  vegetable stock
12 juicy green olives, stoned
  and chopped
4 Tbsp anchovy fillets, drained
  and finely chopped
2 Tbsp chopped fresh parsley

This is a rich sauce to serve with meaty fish such as tuna or swordfish.

I like to add anchovies to cut through the richness, but leave them out

if you must. The longer you cook this the better.

**Preparation time: 10 minutes Cooking time: 35 minutes**

Toss the onions in the oil in a large frying pan, then add plenty of salt and pepper, the leaves from the thyme, and the lemon zest. Cook over a medium heat for 20 minutes until the onions are well softened and starting to brown.

Add the stock, bring to the boil and simmer gently for 5 to 10 minutes until just slightly reduced.

Stir in the olives and anchovies, then season the sauce to taste, adding the parsley and lemon juice at the last moment. Served with grilled fish steaks.

# red onion *and shallot marmalade*

*Makes about 900 g
(2 lb)*

1 kg (2¼ lb) red onions
250 g (9 oz) shallots
100 mL (3½ fl oz) olive oil
6 large sprigs thyme
200 g (7 oz) granulated sugar,
  unrefined if possible
2 tsp coarse sea salt
1 tsp black pepper
100 mL (3½ fl oz) sherry vinegar
350 mL (12 fl oz) Oloroso
  sherry
Lemon juice to taste

A condiment for garnishing chops and steaks and to serve with cold meats

and cheese. The marmalade keeps for about a month in the fridge.

**Preparation time: 15 minutes Cooking time: 1½ hours**

Thinly slice the peeled onions and shallots – the slicing attachment on a food processor does this with the minimum of tears.

Heat the oil in a large deep frying pan, add the onions, shallots and thyme and cook for 25 to 30 minutes, until well softened.

Stir in the sugar, salt and pepper and cook for a further 10 minutes, then add the vinegar and sherry.

Simmer the marmalade for 30 to 40 minutes, until it is thick and most of the liquid has reduced. Season to taste with lemon juice.

Pack into freshly sterilized jars, then seal and label. Refrigerate after opening.

*red onion and shallot marmalade*

# spring onion *and parsley sauce*

This is cream based and rather richer than a traditional white sauce,

but it is bright in taste and colour and is excellent with white fish

like roast cod or grilled skate.

**Preparation time: 10 minutes Cooking time: 10 minutes**

Cook the whites of the onions in the oil in a small frying pan for 6 to 8 minutes over a medium heat until well softened – add the chilli with the spring onions if using.

Pour in the cream and bring the sauce to the boil. Simmer for 2 to 3 minutes, until the cream is just starting to reduce.

Stir in the shredded spring onion greens and the parsley, then season to taste. Add any fish liquor that you have, then serve the sauce spooned over the fish.

*Serves 4 to 6*

8 to 10 spring onions, the
  whites finely chopped and the
  greens shredded lengthways
2 Tbsp groundnut or
  sunflower oil
1 green chilli, finely chopped
  (optional)
250 mL (9 fl oz) double cream
1 large handful (about
  5 Tbsp freshly chopped flat
  leaf parsley)
Salt and paprika

# sage and *red onion stuffing*

*Serves 4 to 6*

2 large handfuls fresh sage

2 large red onions, very finely
   chopped

4 Tbsp butter

175 g (6 oz) fresh white
   breadcrumbs

Salt and black pepper

1 large egg, beaten

This is one of the classic stuffing or forcemeat mixtures, traditionally served with pork. Commercial stuffings are generally made with dried sage and, to my taste, lack colour and pungency. Fresh herbs and a strong onion flavour are essential.

**Preparation time: 25 minutes Cooking time: 30 minutes**

Pour boiling water over the sage leaves in a bowl and leave to stand for 10 minutes.

Fry the onions gently in the butter for about 10 minutes until well softened, then add them and all their juices to the breadcrumbs in a large bowl.

Drain the sage, shake the leaves, then pat dry on kitchen paper. Chop very finely and add to the onions and breadcrumbs with plenty of seasoning.

Add just enough egg to make a moist stuffing that will hold together. Use either to fill a joint of pork, or roll the stuffing into 12 balls. If the stuffing is to be cooked separately, coat the balls in oil or melted butter, then roast them in a hot oven at 200°C/400°F/Gas Mark 6 for 30 minutes, turning and basting them once.

# spiced chickpea *and onion stuffing*

This is a marvellous stuffing to use in a shoulder of lamb.

Ask your butcher to remove the blade bone, then use this stuffing

to fill the cavity. Spice the lamb with ground cumin and

allspice and you'll have a very exotic roast.

**Preparation time: 20 minutes**

Cook the onions in the oil with the chilli powder for 10 minutes, or until softened. Add the aubergine and cook for a further 5 minutes.

Turn the drained chickpeas into a bowl and mash them lightly with the back of a fork. Add the onion and aubergine mixture and stir it throughout the chickpeas. Season well, then use to stuff lamb. This stuffing needs to be cooked in meat as it will not hold together to be roasted in balls.

*Serves 4 to 6*

1 large red onion
6 to 8 spring onions, finely chopped
2 Tbsp chilli or groundnut oil
1 tsp mild chilli powder
1 medium aubergine, finely diced
400 g (14 oz) can chickpeas, drained
Salt and black pepper

# lemon grass, coriander *and onion stuffing*

*Serves 4 to 6*

2 large red onions, finely
chopped

2 Tbsp groundnut oil

Pinch of chilli powder

2 stalks lemon grass, bruised
and very finely chopped

175 g (6 oz) fresh white
breadcrumbs

2 big handfuls chopped fresh
coriander

Salt and black pepper

1 large egg, beaten

4 Tbsp butter, melted

Chopped fresh coriander to
garnish

I like to serve this with baked pork chops. I love stuffings when the outside is
crisp and the inside holds a surprise flavour such as lemon grass.

**Preparation time: 25 minutes Cooking time: 30 minutes**

Preheat the oven to 200°C/400°F/Gas Mark 6.

Cook the onions in the oil with the chilli and lemon grass for 8 to 10 minutes until
well softened. Allow to cool slightly.

Mix the breadcrumbs with the coriander in a large bowl, then season well. Stir the
spiced onions throughout the mixture, add the beaten egg then mix to bind the
stuffing together. Add a little melted butter if necessary to keep the mixture together.

Shape the stuffing into 12 balls – wet your hands with cold water to make the
shaping easier.

Melt the butter in a suitable roasting pan on the stove, then add the stuffing balls
and turn them in the butter until completely coated. Roast in the hot oven for about
30 minutes, until a deep golden brown. Sprinkle with extra coriander and serve with
oven-baked pork chops.

# soups, starters & hors d'oeuvres

*The star of the starter or an essential background flavouring?*
*Onions can dominate and enrich soups and starters or be*
*used as a piquant last-minute garnish.*

# french onion *soup*

*Serves 6*

1 Tbsp butter

2 Tbsp olive oil

4 large onions, finely sliced

700mL (1¼ pints) beef or
 vegetable stock

Salt and black pepper

3 to 4 large bay leaves

6 thick slices French bread

85 g (3 oz) grated Swiss cheese

The traditional hangover-remedy soup, sold in all-night cafés in Paris to revive revellers in the early hours of the morning. Some people thicken this soup with flour, but I like it just as it is.

**Preparation time: 30–40 minutes Cooking time: 30–40 minutes**

Heat the butter and oil together in a large pan, add the onions and cook over a medium heat for about 20 to 30 minutes until well browned but not burned.

Add the stock to the pan, along with the seasonings. Bring to the boil, cover and simmer for 30 minutes.

Remove the bay leaves, then season again to taste.

Place the bread, either in the soup in a heatproof serving dish or on a grill rack. Scatter with the cheese and grill until just browned. Serve the toasted bread floating in the soup.

# lebanese onion *and couscous soup*

*Serves 6*

4 large onions, finely sliced

2 Tbsp oil

1 Tbsp butter

1 red chilli, seeded and
 finely chopped

1 tsp mild chilli powder

½ tsp ground turmeric

1 tsp ground coriander

2 L (3½ pints) vegetable or
 chicken stock

Salt and black pepper

55 g (2 oz) couscous

Similar to French onion soup but with extra spice, this is especially good for really cold days.

**Preparation time: 20 minutes Cooking time: 40 minutes**

Cook the onions in the oil and butter until well browned – this will take about 15 minutes over a medium heat.

Stir in the chopped chilli and the spices and cook over a low heat for a further 1 to 2 minutes before adding the stock. Season lightly then bring to the boil. Cover and simmer for 30 minutes.

Stir the couscous into the soup, bring back to the boil and simmer for a further 10 minutes. Season to taste and serve immediately.

*french onion soup*

# cauliflower *and spring onion soup*

*Serves 4 to 6*

1 bunch spring onions (about 8 to 10), trimmed

2 Tbsp butter

1 large potato, peeled and diced

1 large cauliflower, chopped (including the stalk)

1.2 L (2 pints) water

Salt and black pepper

250 mL (9 fl oz) milk, or more

A thick vegetable soup, the green onion tops providing an appealing garnish.

No herbs, spices or stock are required – the flavour of the cauliflower and the onions is more than enough.

**Preparation time: 10 minutes Cooking time: 30 minutes**

Reserve the green tops of the spring onions. Chop the white part and add to the butter in a pan and cook slowly for 5 minutes, until the onions are softened.

Stir in the potato and cauliflower, cover and cook over a low heat for a further 5 minutes, shaking the pan from time to time.

Add the water with the salt and pepper and bring to the boil. Cover the pan, then simmer for 20 minutes.

Remove from the heat and allow the soup to cool slightly then purée until smooth. Return to the stove and add the milk, thinning the soup to the required consistency. Reheat gently, seasoning to taste.

Finely chop the reserved green onion tops and stir into the soup just before serving.

# chilled spring onion *and cucumber*

Its lively flavours make this a soup to be enjoyed by everyone,

even those who claim not to like chilled soups.

**Preparation time: 1½ hours, including cooling time Chilling time: about 2 hours**

Reserve a few of the green onion tops for the garnish, then place the remaining onions, lemon grass, chillies and lime leaves in a large pan with the crumbled stock cube. Add the water, then bring to the boil. Add the cucumber, cover the pan and remove it immediately from the heat. Allow to marinate for 1 hour.

Purée the soup until smooth, then press the mixture through a fine sieve with the back of a ladle. Whisk in the yoghurt and fish sauce, then season to taste with a little salt if necessary. Chill thoroughly for at least 2 hours.

Add the reserved chopped onion tops to the soup just before serving and spoon the soup over a tablespoon or so of crushed ice in each bowl to serve.

*Serves 6*

6 large spring onions, trimmed
   and sliced
1 stalk lemon grass, bruised
   and finely chopped
2 green chillies and 2 caribe
   chillies, or 3 green chillies,
   seeded and finely chopped
2 lime leaves or finely grated
   zest of 1 lime
1 vegetable stock cube, crumbled
850 mL (1½ pints) water
1 large cucumber, seeded and
   chopped
250 mL (9 fl oz) natural
   yoghurt
1 Tbsp fish sauce
Salt to taste

# roast red onion *and pepper soup*

*Serves 4 to 6*

2 large red onions, peeled and
   halved
1 large red pepper and
   1 large green pepper
Salt and black pepper
About 4–5 Tbsp olive oil
14 oz (400 g) can chopped
   tomatoes
700 mL (1¼ pints) vegetable or
   chicken stock
Handful of basil leaves
2 Tbsp pesto or *tapénade* (black
   olive paste)
Shavings of Parmesan cheese
   to serve

Redolent in flavours of the Mediterranean, this rich soup is a meal in itself

served with crusty bread.

**Preparation time: 1 hour Cooking time: 20 minutes**

Preheat the oven to 220°C/425°F/Gas Mark 7. Place the onions and peppers on a baking sheet, season lightly then drizzle with a little olive oil. Roast for about 40 minutes, until the peppers are blackened – turn them once during cooking. Cover the peppers with a damp dish towel and leave for 10 minutes or so, once cooked – this helps to steam loose the skins.

Peel and core the peppers, then roughly chop them with the onions. Cook in the remaining oil for 2 to 3 minutes, then add the tomatoes and stock. Bring to the boil then add the basil and seasonings. Cover and simmer for 15 minutes.

Purée the soup until smooth, return to the pan, and reheat gently if necessary, seasoning to taste. Add a little more stock or water if the soup is too thick.

Swirl the pesto or *tapénade* into the soup, and garnish with Parmesan shavings just before serving.

# english–style *onion soup*

*Serves 4 to 6*

4 Tbsp butter
1 Tbsp olive oil
3 large onions, finely sliced
2 Tbsp plain flour
1.2 L (2 pints) vegetable stock
Salt and black pepper
½ tsp ground mace
250 mL (9 fl oz) milk
Lemon juice to taste

A smooth flavoursome soup that's great after a

digging session in the garden.

**Preparation time: 30-40 minutes Cooking time: 30-40 minutes**

Heat the butter and oil together in a large pan, add the onions and cook over a moderate heat for about 20 minutes, until well browned. It is important to brown and not burn the onions, and to achieve a good rich chestnut-brown colour, or the soup will be insipid.

Stir in the flour, then cook for 2 to 3 minutes until well browned before gradually stirring in the stock.

Bring to the boil, add the seasonings, cover and cook for 30 to 40 minutes.

Stir in the milk then season the soup to taste, adding a little lemon juice. Reheat gently and serve with crusty bread and strong cheese.

# onion, squash *and coconut soup*

This smooth, spicy soup has a very unusual flavour.

The yoghurt provides a cooling garnish.

*Serves 4 to 6*

2 large onions, sliced

2 Tbsp sunflower or groundnut oil

500 g (1 lb 2 oz) prepared
squash, such as butternut,
finely diced

1 to 2 stalks lemon grass,
finely chopped

3 small Thai red chillies, seeded
if wished and finely chopped

3 kaffir lime leaves, finely grated
or shredded zest of 2 limes

1.2 L (2 pints) vegetable stock

Salt and black pepper

125 mL (4 fl oz) coconut milk
or cream

2 Tbsp fish sauce

yoghurt and chopped coriander
to serve

**Preparation time: 15 minutes Cooking time: 40 minutes**

Cook the onions in the oil in a covered pan for 10 minutes, until softened but not
browned. Add the squash and cook for a further 5 minutes.

Stir in the lemon grass, chillies, and lime leaves or zest, then add the stock and bring
to the boil. Season lightly, cover and simmer for 20 minutes, or until the squash is tender.

Cool slightly, add the coconut milk and fish sauce then blend the soup to a smooth
purée. Season to taste with salt – if you have left the chilli seeds in it is very unlikely
you will need pepper!

Serve with a spoonful of natural yoghurt and chopped coriander.

# poppy seed *onion rings*

*Serves 2*

Oil to deep-fry
85 g (3 oz) plain flour
2 Tbsp poppy seeds
1 Tbsp white mustard seeds
Salt and black pepper
2 large onions, cut into
  1.25 cm (½ in) slices
A little milk

I don't always feel like making a batter when I fancy some onion rings, so this crisp flour coating makes an ideal alternative. The poppy and mustard seeds provide a good contrast to the soft texture of the onion.

**Preparation time: 10 minutes Cooking time: 15 minutes**

Heat the oil to 180°C/350°F in a large pan or a deep-fryer.
  Mix together all the dry ingredients. Separate the onion slices into rings.
  Dip the rings into a little milk, then toss them in the spiced flour. Prepare the rings in about 3 batches, just before frying them.
  Carefully lower the onion rings, a few at a time, into the hot oil. Fry for 3 to 4 minutes until golden brown, then scoop them out with a slotted spoon and drain on crumpled kitchen paper. Repeat until all the rings are fried.
  Serve as a side dish, or on a bed of salad leaves as a quick snack.

# spiced *onion balls*

*Makes about 24*

Oil to deep-fry
175 g (6 oz) wholemeal flour
1 tsp salt
½ tsp bicarbonate of soda
1 Tbsp ground rice
1 Tbsp mild curry powder
1 tsp chilli powder
1 small green chilli, seeded and
  finely chopped
2 large onions, finely sliced
250 mL (9 fl oz) water

These fried onion balls are best made with very fine besan or chickpea flour, but I am using a very fine wholemeal flour, the type that is fine enough for pastry, which is more widely available. Don't make them too big, or they will not cook through in the centre before burning.

**Preparation time: 10 minutes Cooking time: about 20 minutes**

Heat the oil in a deep-fryer to 170°C/330°F.
  Mix all the dry ingredients together in a bowl, then add the chilli powder and chopped chilli and onions. Add more onion if necessary; there should be more onion than spiced flour.
  Gradually add sufficient water to obtain a soft, thick paste.
  Carefully lower heaped teaspoonfuls of mixture into the hot oil and fry for about 10 minutes, until browned and crisp.
  Drain thoroughly on kitchen paper and serve with chutney or onion, radish or cucumber raita (see page 50).

# onion rings *in beer-batter*

A delicious batter for the ever-popular fried onion rings. Beer gives the batter

an excellent flavour, and the addition of egg white keeps it crisp and light.

*Serves 2*

Oil to deep-fry
85 g (3 oz) plain flour
3 Tbsp corn or vegetable oil
250 mL (9 fl oz) beer
1 large egg white
2 large red onions, cut into
  1 cm (½ inch) slices

**Preparation time: 15 minutes Cooking time: 10 minutes**

Heat the oil to 190°C/375°F in a large pan or a deep-fryer.

Blend the flour with the oil and beer in a bowl. Whisk the egg white until stiff, then fold it into the batter just before using – this is easiest with a wire whisk.

Separate the onion slices into rings. Coat them in the batter just before frying, then lower them carefully into the hot oil. Fry the rings for 3 to 4 minutes until golden brown, turning them over as necessary.

Remove the rings from the oil with a slotted spoon and drain them on crumpled kitchen paper. Continue cooking in batches.

Serve with steaks, grilled fish or as a simple snack on their own with a garlic or tomato dip.

# spring onion *rolls*

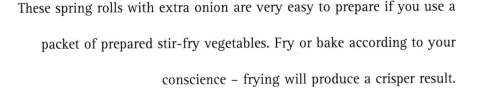

*Serves 4*

300 g (10½ oz) prepared mixed
  stir-fry vegetables
6 spring onions, cut into 5 cm
  (2 in) pieces then finely sliced
  lengthways
8 or 16 sheets filo pastry,
  according to size
Groundnut oil to brush
Oil to deep-fry
Chilli dipping sauce to serve

These spring rolls with extra onion are very easy to prepare if you use a packet of prepared stir-fry vegetables. Fry or bake according to your conscience – frying will produce a crisper result.

**Preparation time: 20 minutes Cooking time: about 12 minutes**

Mix the prepared stir-fry vegetables with the spring onions. Preheat the oven to 220°C/425°F/Gas Mark 7 if you are going to bake the rolls.

Prepare the filo pastry – you need 8 stacks of 15 cm (6 in) squares of filo, 4 sheets thick. Brush each sheet with oil before stacking.

Divide the vegetables among the pastry. Fold the bases up over the filling and fold in the sides, then roll up, sealing the edges firmly. It is very important to seal the edges if you are going to fry the rolls, otherwise they will unwrap and the filling will ooze out. A dab of water will 'glue' the pastry.

Bake the rolls for 10 to 12 minutes in a hot oven, or deep-fry them 4 at a time in hot oil at 190°C/375°F for 3 to 4 minutes, until golden brown. Turn carefully once during cooking. Drain the fried rolls well on plenty of crumpled kitchen paper.

Serve with a small salad or herb garnish and plenty of chilli dipping sauce.

# onion, rosemary *and gorgonzola crostini*

*Serves 4*

1 large shallot
16 prepared cocktail toast
  squares
4 spring onions, finely chopped
1 Tbsp chopped fresh rosemary
2 sun-dried tomatoes, finely
  chopped
115 g (4 oz) crumbled
  Gorgonzola
Salt and black pepper

A crispy hors d'oeuvre to serve with drinks. I rub the prepared toasts with the cut surface of a shallot for extra onion flavour. Using prepared cocktail toasts cuts down on preparation time.

**Preparation time: 15 minutes Cooking time: 5 minutes**

Cut the shallot in half and rub the surface over the toasts, then finely chop the shallot and place it in a bowl with the remaining ingredients. Mix well.

Preheat the grill. Divide the topping among the flavoured toasts, then grill them until the cheese is just starting to melt and brown. Serve immediately.

# tomato *and spring onion bruschettas*

These toasts have a scent of the Mediterranean about them, and the spring

onions used here make a welcome change from the more typical garlic.

Add mozzarella cheese if you wish, to make a more substantial snack.

Preparation time: 30 minutes Cooking time: 10 minutes

*Serves 2*

Slice the tomatoes and place them in a bowl with the spring onions. Season well, then add the oil and leave for 20 minutes, stirring from time to time.

Toast one side of the bread under a grill, then turn it over and pile on the tomatoes and spring onions. Reserve the olive oil. Grill until the tomatoes start to blacken – make sure all the bread is covered or it will burn.

Spoon the oil over the *bruschettas* and garnish with a small lettuce leaf or other greens to serve.

2 to 3 ripe plum tomatoes
2 spring onions, finely sliced
Salt and black pepper
2 Tbsp olive oil
4 to 6 slices French bread, or
  2 slices wholemeal bread

# cheese *and onion beignets*

*Makes about 15*

Oil to deep-fry
4 Tbsp butter
150 mL (5 fl oz) water
55 g (2 oz) plain flour
2 medium eggs, beaten
55 g (2 oz) grated Cheddar
  cheese
1 shallot, minced
Salt and cayenne pepper

These fried pastry puffs are really easy to make, but it is important to measure the ingredients accurately. Add the egg to the dough gradually; you may not need it all. You want the dough to hold its shape, so keep it quite stiff.

**Preparation time: 15 minutes Cooking time: 10-12 minutes**

Preheat the oil in a deep-fryer to 200°C/400°F.

To make the choux pastry, heat the butter and water together in a saucepan until the butter has melted, then bring to the rolling boil. Add the flour all at once – I usually sieve it on to a piece of greaseproof paper to make it easier to tip into the pan. Immediately take the pan off the heat and beat vigorously, until the mixture forms a ball and leaves the sides of the pan. A sturdy wooden spoon works best.

Gradually add the beaten eggs, beating well between each addition, until they are well mixed into the dough, then add the cheese, shallot and seasoning.

Carefully drop teaspoonfuls of the choux pastry into the hot fat and deep-fry for 3 to 4 minutes, until golden brown. Drain thoroughly on plenty of crumpled kitchen paper and serve hot.

# roast onion *and aubergine pâté*

*Serves 6*

1 large onion
1 medium aubergine
Salt and black pepper
Olive oil
225 g (8 oz) cream cheese
1 garlic clove
Pinch of chilli powder
Lemon or lime juice to taste

This makes an excellent dip or spread, alternatively try it folded in tortillas.

**Preparation time: 15 minutes Cooking time: 45 minutes, plus cooling time**

Preheat the oven to 220°C/425°F/Gas Mark 7.

Cut the onion into quarters and place on a baking sheet with the aubergine. Season lightly, then drizzle with olive oil. Roast in the hot oven for 45 minutes, until the aubergine is blackened and the skin wrinkled. Allow to cool.

Cut off and discard the end of the aubergine. Place the aubergine in a food processor with the onion, cream cheese, garlic and chilli powder and blend until completely smooth.

Season the pâté with salt and pepper and lemon or lime juice to taste.

*soups, starters*
*& hors d'oeuvres*

*cheese and onion beignets*

# onion *and chicken satay skewers*

*Serves 4*

Small piece fresh root ginger

2 shallots, chopped

2 stalks lemon grass, bruised
and finely chopped

2 Tbsp satay (peanut) sauce

1 tsp ground turmeric

1 Tbsp demerara sugar

½ tsp salt

Water

450 g (1 lb) chicken breast
fillets or pork tenderloin,
trimmed and very finely sliced

Probably one of the best foods for the barbecue! Soak the bamboo sticks in water to stop them scorching during cooking. This is also delicious made from chicken or pork.

**Preparation time: 15 minutes, plus 2 hours marinating Cooking time: about 10 minutes**

Grate the ginger, gather up the pieces in your hand, then squeeze the juice into a small blender or jug. Add the shallots, lemon grass, satay sauce, turmeric, sugar and salt. Blend until smooth, adding a little water if necessary.

Shred the chicken or pork, then marinate in the sauce in a small bowl for 2 hours. Turn the meat in the sauce once or twice.

Soak 16 wooden skewers in cold water for 30 minutes while the meat is marinating.

Thread the strips on to the skewers – do not pack too tightly, so the meat can cook through quickly.

Cook the skewers for 3 to 4 minutes on each side, either over a medium-hot barbecue or under a grill. The cooking time will depend on the thickness of the meat. Serve hot, with a cucumber and chilli salad.

# salads

*Stir-fried in cinnamon, chopped into cracked wheat or dressings, or teamed with hot duck or pickled herrings, onions and salads are perfect partners, with the versatile bulbs adding flavour, bite and freshness.*

# onion *raita*

*Serves 4*

1 onion, finely sliced
2 Tbsp vegetable oil
1 tsp cumin seeds
1 red onion, finely sliced
1 small red chilli, seeded and
  finely chopped (optional)
2–3 Tbsp chopped fresh
  coriander
350 g (12 oz) natural yoghurt
Salt and black pepper

A refreshing salad to serve with fried dishes, or with plain-cooked steak.

It is also a cooling accompaniment to many Indian dishes.

**Preparation time: 5 minutes Cooking time: 5 minutes**

Cook the onion in the oil for about 3 to 4 minutes until softened but not browned. Add the cumin seeds and cook for a further 2 to 3 minutes until golden brown. Turn into a serving bowl.

Add all the remaining ingredients, seasoning well to taste. Allow to stand for 10 to 15 minutes before serving, if possible, to allow the flavours to blend.

*salads*

# tomato *and onion salsa*

A simple salsa that relies on a variety of tomatoes and onions for its flavour and colour.

Preparation time: 15 minutes

Heat a small non-stick frying pan then add the cumin seeds and cook for 30 seconds or so, until fragrant. Turn on to a chopping board and crush lightly with the end of a rolling pin, then scrape into a bowl.

Add the prepared tomatoes and onions.

Season lightly, then add the oil and vinegar and toss the salsa together. Allow to stand for at least an hour before stirring in the parsley and serving.

*Serves 4*

1 tsp cumin seeds
2 red and 2 yellow tomatoes, chopped
8 cherry or baby plum tomatoes, halved
1 red onion, chopped
6 spring onions, trimmed and chopped
Salt and black pepper
2 Tbsp olive oil
1 Tbsp white wine vinegar
2 Tbsp chopped fresh parsley

# four-onion *salsa*

For real onion addicts! This is very good served with poppadoms before an Indian meal. The heat of the onions is balanced by the cool yoghurt.

Preparation time: 15 minutes

Heat a small frying pan, then add the onion seeds and dry-fry for 30 seconds or so, until just fragrant. Turn into a bowl.

Add the onions to the seeds and season well.

Blend the yoghurt and soured cream together, then spoon into the onions and mix well. Serve as an accompaniment to spicy dishes.

*Serves 4*

2 Tbsp onion seeds
2 red onions, finely sliced
4 spring onions, trimmed and finely sliced
4 silverskin onions or mild shallots, cut into 6 or 8 pieces
Salt and black pepper
115 g (4 oz) natural yoghurt
125 mL (4 fl oz) soured cream

# tomato and *apricot salad with cinnamon-fried onions*

*Serves 4*

55 g (2 oz) blanched almonds

2 large onions, finely sliced

2 Tbsp olive oil

1 tsp ground cinnamon

Salad leaves

4 ripe tomatoes, cut into wedges

225 g (8 oz) ready-to-eat dried apricots, chopped

Salt and black pepper

Chopped fresh parsley to garnish

Tomatoes and moist dried apricots make a flavoursome salad, especially when topped with cinnamon-fried onions. This is great with an aubergine or chickpea dip, and lots of warmed flat breads.

**Preparation time: 15 minutes Cooking time: 10 minutes**

Heat a large frying pan, add the almonds and cook them for 2 to 3 minutes, until lightly browned. Turn into a bowl and leave to cool.

Cook the onions in the oil with the cinnamon – use the same frying pan again. Cook for 5 to 6 minutes, until the onions are softened and starting to brown.

Meanwhile, arrange the salad leaves in a bowl and top with the tomatoes and apricots. Season lightly.

Season the onions, then tip them into the centre of the salad, with all their juices. Mix together, sprinkle generously with parsley and serve immediately.

# herring *and mixed onion salad*

Onions mixed with herrings and soured cream is a typical Scandinavian cold-table dish which is great for brunch or lunch. You can add any roe to this – fry it with the herrings for 2 to 3 minutes.

**Preparation time: 20 minutes Cooking time: about 10 minutes**

Season the herring fillets well, then turn them in the flour to coat.

Heat the oil in a large frying pan, add the fillets skin side up and cook for 3 to 4 minutes, depending on size.

Meanwhile, arrange the lettuce and watercress on plates. Toss the apple in lemon juice and arrange on the leaves.

Turn the herrings and cook for a further 2 to 3 minutes (add any roe at this stage, if using).

Arrange the onion rings on the salad.

Cut the herrings into bite-size pieces and arrange on the salad. Add the soured cream, top with the chopped spring onions and serve.

*Serves 4*

4 large herrings or 2 mackerel, filleted
Salt and black pepper
4 Tbsp oat flour or wholemeal flour
3 Tbsp groundnut oil
2 heads butterhead lettuce, washed and broken into bite-size pieces
2 handfuls watercress
1 large apple, cored and sliced
1 Tbsp lemon juice
1 red onion, cut into rings
4 Tbsp soured cream
1 to 2 spring onions, trimmed and finely chopped

# onion and wild *mushroom salad*

*Serves 2*

1 medium onion, chopped

3 Tbsp olive oil

280 g (10 oz) wild mushrooms, trimmed and thickly sliced

Salt and black pepper

2 Tbsp chopped fresh parsley

Salad leaves to serve

1 Tbsp shallot or sherry vinegar

If wild mushrooms are unavailable, use ordinary cultivated ones.

If gathering your own wild mushrooms, exercise great care; many varieties are inedible and poisonous.

Preparation time: 10 minutes Cooking time: 10 minutes

In a frying pan over a low heat, cook the onion in the olive oil for about 4 to 5 minutes until softened and translucent.

Add less-tender mushrooms to the pan first and cook for 2 minutes. Add all the remaining mushrooms and sauté slowly until just soft, about 3 minutes.

Season to taste, then add plenty of chopped parsley. Remove the mushrooms from the pan with a slotted spoon and pile on to beds of mixed salad leaves on individual serving plates.

Add the vinegar to the juices in the frying pan – add a little more oil if necessary. Bring to the boil, spoon over the salad and serve immediately.


# onion and *orange salsa*

*Serves 4*

1 orange

2 tomatoes, chopped

¹/₂ red onion

4 spring onions, finely chopped

1 small green chilli, seeded and finely chopped

2 Tbsp chopped fresh coriander

1 green pepper, seeded and shredded

Salt and black pepper

Salad leaves to serve (optional)

This is good served with salad leaves, and also spooned over thick bean soups or as a garnish to bean casseroles.

Preparation time: 20 minutes

Pare a few strands of rind from the orange and reserve for garnish. Cut away all the pith and membrane from the orange, then cut the flesh into good-size chunks, removing any seeds.

Mix the orange with all the remaining ingredients, seasoning well. Allow to stand for at least an hour, then serve on a bed of salad leaves if you wish.

# onion, orange *and tomato salad*

My favourite salad to serve with fish dishes. I have included a recipe for a vinaigrette which complements it perfectly.

**Preparation time: 15 minutes**

Arrange the rocket, watercress and chicory in a large bowl. Cut the orange segments in half, remove any seeds then toss them in with the tomatoes and spring onions. Season lightly.

Whisk all the vinaigrette ingredients together until thoroughly blended. Spoon over the salad, mix and serve.

*Serves 4*

2 handfuls rocket
2 handfuls watercress
2 heads chicory, trimmed and
  finely sliced
1 orange, peeled and divided
  into segments
4 ripe tomatoes, cut into
  wedges
6 spring onions, trimmed and
  finely chopped
Salt and black pepper

VINAIGRETTE
4 Tbsp olive oil
1 Tbsp white wine vinegar
1 Tbsp Dijon mustard
Salt, black pepper and lemon
  juice to taste

# hot chinese duck *and onion salad*

*Serves 2*

Coarse sea salt

2 duckling breast fillets

8 to 10 spring onions, trimmed

2.5 cm (1 in) piece fresh root
ginger, peeled and shredded

1 garlic clove, finely chopped

2 fresh red chillies, finely
shredded

½ Chinese cabbage (pak choi),
shredded

2 small heads Chinese leaves,
trimmed and shredded

1 Tbsp sesame seeds

4 Tbsp dark soy sauce

2 Tbsp dry sherry

This elegant salad is almost a cross between a salad and a stir-fry and

I can heartily recommend it!

**Preparation time: 10 minutes Cooking time: 40 minutes**

Preheat the oven to 220°C/425°F/Gas Mark 7. Rub a little sea salt into the fat of the duck then roast the breast fillets in the hot oven for 25 to 30 minutes, depending on how pink you like the meat.

Cut deeply lengthways into both ends of 4 to 6 spring onions. Place in a bowl of cold water to curl. Roughly chop the remaining spring onions.

Prepare all the remaining vegetables.

Heat a wok, add the sesame seeds and dry-fry for a few seconds until toasted. Reserve until required.

Allow the duck to stand for 5 minutes or so, spooning off 2 tablespoons of the fat into the hot wok. Quickly stir-fry the ginger and garlic for a few seconds until fragrant, then add the chopped spring onions and cook for a further 1 minute. Stir in the chillies, cabbage and Chinese leaves and stir-fry for a further 2 to 3 minutes. Add the sesame seeds and a good pinch of salt, toss well then scoop out with a slotted spoon and pile on to two warmed plates.

Add the soy sauce to the wok with the sherry and bring to the boil. Meanwhile, quickly shred the duck meat and scatter it over the vegetables. Pour the dressing over the salad, then garnish with the onion curls. Serve immediately.

*hot chinese duck and onion salad*

# mexican *onion salad*

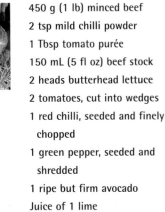

*Serves 3 to 4*

450 g (1 lb) minced beef

2 tsp mild chilli powder

1 Tbsp tomato purée

150 mL (5 fl oz) beef stock

2 heads butterhead lettuce

2 tomatoes, cut into wedges

1 red chilli, seeded and finely
  chopped

1 green pepper, seeded and
  shredded

1 ripe but firm avocado

Juice of 1 lime

2-3 Tbsp vinaigrette

1 red onion, cut into fine rings

Tortilla chips to serve

A main course salad that needs no accompaniment –

other than a cold beer.

**Preparation time: 15 minutes Cooking time: 30 minutes, plus 30 minutes to cool**

Brown the minced beef in a non-stick frying pan, then add the chilli powder and tomato purée with the stock and bring to the boil. Simmer for 20 minutes, then allow to cool.

Arrange the lettuce on a large platter, then top with the minced beef. Arrange the tomatoes, chilli and pepper over the beef.

Peel the avocado, remove the stone then slice. Toss the pieces in the lime juice, then arrange them over the salad.

Drizzle lightly with the vinaigrette dressing, then top with the red onion slices. Serve with tortilla chips.

# mixed pickle *salad*

*Serves 4*

6 cooked new potatoes,
  chopped

250 g (9 oz) mixed pickles
  including onions, gherkins,
  and bell peppers

1 red onion, chopped

6 spring onions, trimmed and
  chopped

Salt and black pepper

About 4 Tbsp mayonnaise

A salad accompaniment – just a couple of spoonfuls is all you need – to

brighten up even the dullest of leftovers.

**Preparation time: 10 minutes**

Place the chopped potatoes in a bowl. Roughly chop the pickles and add them to the potatoes with the onions and a little seasoning.

Stir in just enough mayonnaise to moisten the salad before serving.

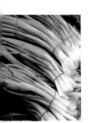

# onion *caponata*

*Caponata* is generally thought of as an aubergine-based dish, but here it is made extra special by the addition of onions.

*Serves 4*

**Preparation time: 45 minutes Cooking time: 30 minutes**

Layer the diced aubergine in a colander with salt, then allow to stand for 30 minutes. Rinse thoroughly in cold water, shake well, and pat dry on kitchen paper.

Pour most of the oil into a large frying pan, add the aubergine and cook until browned and soft, which will take 10 to 12 minutes. In a separate pan, cook the onions, pickles, capers and olives slowly in the remaining oil over a very low heat for about 10 minutes, until softened. Add the sugar and vinegar and continue to cook slowly until the smell of the vinegar has gone.

Drain any excess oil from the aubergine, then add it to the other vegetables with the pine nuts. Add a little salt to season, if necessary. Serve warm or cold.

2 large aubergines, trimmed and cut into 1.25 cm ($\frac{1}{2}$ in) dice
Salt
125 mL (4 fl oz) light olive oil
2 red onions, sliced
28 g (9 oz) mixed pickled vegetables (onions, gherkins, pickled peppers, etc.), chopped
40 g ($1\frac{1}{2}$ oz) capers
55 g (2 oz) stoned green olives
1 Tbsp sugar
150 mL (5 fl oz) red wine vinegar
2 Tbsp pine nuts

# spiced beef *and onion salad*

*Serves 2*

3 Tbsp chilli or groundnut oil

175 g (6 oz) lean boneless beef, thinly sliced then cut into 2 cm (³/₄ in) strips

3 small heads Chinese leaves, sliced thick

1 large carrot, julienned

6 spring onions, cut into 4 cm (1¹/₂ in) pieces

1 Tbsp chopped pickled ginger

1 tsp hot fresh chilli paste

Soy sauce and salt to taste

Salad leaves to serve

Wafer-thin strips of beef for stir-fries make this a very quick salad to prepare – but tastes as if you have spent hours in the kitchen.

Preparation time: 10 minutes Cooking time: about 5 minutes

Heat a wok, add the oil then stir-fry the beef for 1 to 2 minutes. Add the stalks of the Chinese leaves with the carrot and spring onions and stir-fry for a further 2 minutes.

Add the pickled ginger and chilli paste with the Chinese leaves and cook for a further 1 minute.

Season the stir-fry with soy sauce and salt to taste, then spoon over a bed of salad leaves with all the pan juices and serve immediately.

# onion *coleslaw*

*Serves 6*

¹/₂ small green cabbage, shredded

3 large carrots, peeled and grated

1 red onion, finely chopped

4 spring onions, trimmed and finely sliced

Salt and black pepper

125 mL (4 fl oz) mayonnaise

6 Tbsp natural yoghurt

Coleslaw should always include a generous amount of onion. It is often better the day after it is made, when the flavours have had a chance to blend.

Preparation time: 15 minutes

Mix all the vegetables together in a large bowl and season well.

Add the mayonnaise and yoghurt and mix thoroughly, ensuring that all the vegetables are well coated in the dressing.

# onion *and chilli tabbouleh*

Tabbouleh, a salad of bulgur wheat, is usually flavoured with herbs. In this version I use onions and chillies for a little more spice.

**Preparation time: 40 minutes**

Place the bulgur wheat in a bowl, pour over the boiling water and allow to stand for 30 minutes. Drain, then squeeze dry through a fine sieve or in a clean dish towel.

Turn the bulgur wheat into a large bowl and mix in all the remaining ingredients. Mix well, then serve at room temperature.

*Serves 6*

175 g (6 oz) fine bulgur wheat

450 mL (16 fl oz) boiling water

6 spring onions, finely chopped

1 red and 1 green chilli, finely chopped

½ cucumber, finely diced

1 bunch watercress, chopped

Juice of ½ lemon

Salt and black pepper

4 Tbsp extra virgin olive oil

# shallot caesar *salad*

*Serves 2 as a main course or 4 as a starter*

8 Tbsp freshly grated Parmesan cheese shavings

2 heads butterhead lettuce, rinsed and broken into bite-size pieces

1 large banana shallot or 2 standard ones, finely chopped

2 Tbsp olive oil

2 large eggs, beaten

2-3 Tbsp double cream

Salt and black pepper

For days when you can't live without a Caesar salad but your friend doesn't want garlic! Use the best Parmesan cheese you can find.

Preparation time: 5 minutes Cooking time: 15 minutes

Heat a large non-stick frying pan, then carefully fry the cheese in 8 little mounds for 1½ to 2 minutes, until golden brown and melted together into a crisp. Turn with a spatula and cook the other side. Cool on a wire rack.

Arrange the lettuce in a large bowl.

Cook the chopped shallot in the oil in a pan until softened but not browned. Beat the eggs with the cream and add to the pan. Cook gently until just starting to set.

Break up the Parmesan and add the crisp pieces to the lettuce with plenty of salt and pepper, then pour the egg dressing over. Mix thoroughly and serve immediately.

# meat & fish main courses

*The richness of slow-braised onions blends perfectly with red meat casseroles, while quick-fried or even raw onions can season fish and poultry dishes without dominating. Whether supporting or leading the flavours, the onion is fundamental.*

# beef *and onion pasties*

350 g (12 oz) best stewing
   steak, chuck or blade, cubed
140 g (5 oz) peeled diced
   potato
1 medium onion, finely
   chopped
Salt and black pepper
350 g (12 oz) plain flour, sieved
6 Tbsp butter or margarine
Cold water to mix

A traditional dish in Cornwall – meat and

vegetables held in a pastry casing.

**Preparation time: 45 minutes Cooking time: 1¼ hours**

Preheat the oven to 220°C/425°F/Gas Mark 7. Lightly oil a baking sheet.

   Cut the stewing steak into 6 mm (¼ in) dice, then mix it with the vegetables and season well.

   Mix the flour with a good pinch of salt, then rub in the butter until the mixture resembles fine breadcrumbs. Add just enough cold water to bind the dough, then divide in four. On a lightly floured board roll out each piece into a 20 cm (8 in) circle – use a plate to cut around.

   Divide the filling among the pastry circles, then dampen the edges and bring them together over the filling. Seal them together, then flute the edges decoratively with your fingers. Place on the oiled baking sheet.

   Bake the pasties for 15 minutes, then reduce the temperature to 170°C/325°F/Gas Mark 3 for a further 1 hour. Serve the pasties hot or cold – they are great picnic food.

# poached smoked haddock *with sweet onion cream sauce*

*Serves 4*

2 large sweet onions, thinly
   sliced
2 Tbsp olive oil
4 pieces smoked haddock, each
   weighing about 175 g (6 oz)
150 mL (5 fl oz) vegetable or
   fish stock
3 Tbsp double cream
Salt and black pepper
1–2 Tbsp snipped fresh chives

Onions and fish aren't always perfect partners, but sweet onions complement

the subtle flavour of fish very well.

**Preparation time: 10 minutes Cooking time: 20 minutes**

Cook the onions in the oil for 5 to 8 minutes until softened and a rich golden brown.

   Place the haddock on top of the onions, add the stock, then cover and simmer gently for 5 minutes, or until the fish is just done.

   Carefully lift the fish from the pan and set aside. Remove the onions with a slotted spoon and make nests of them on each of four warmed plates. Arrange the fish on top and keep warm.

   Boil the onion juices until well reduced then stir in the cream. Season the sauce to taste then add the chives. Spoon the sauce over the fish and serve immediately.

*beef and onion pasties*

# sausage, onion *and egg pie*

A comforting winter dish – leftover cooked ham could be used instead of sausages if you wish.

*Serves 6 to 8*

2 large onions, cut into 4 or 6

250 mL (9 fl oz) water

1/2 tsp ground mace or
   2 bay leaves

250 mL (9 fl oz) milk

3 Tbsp butter

2 Tbsp plain flour

Salt and black pepper

6 to 8 thick sausages, cut into
   4 cm (1 1/2 in) chunks

4 hard-boiled eggs, quartered

2 Tbsp capers (optional)

PASTRY

185 g (6 1/2 oz) plain flour

Pinch of salt

2 Tbsp butter

Cold water to mix

Preparation time: 45 minutes Cooking time: 45 minutes

Place the onions in a saucepan with the water and mace or bay leaves. Cover and simmer until tender, about 15 minutes. Remove the flavourings and add the milk, butter and flour. Bring to the boil, stirring continuously until thickened. Season to taste then remove from the heat and allow to cool slightly.

Preheat the oven to 200°C/400°F/Gas Mark 6. Brown the sausages on all sides in a non-stick frying pan. Combine the sauce with the sausages, eggs and capers (if using), then turn into a buttered pie dish.

Mix the flour and salt, then rub in the butter until the mixture resembles fine breadcrumbs. Add sufficient water to bind to a stiff dough, then roll out on a lightly floured board and use to cover the pie. Make a hole in the middle of the pastry with a knife to allow the steam to escape and to keep the pastry crisp, and use any trimmings to make pastry leaves to decorate the pie. Place the pie on a baking sheet, in case some of the filling bubbles over.

Bake in the hot oven for 45 minutes, or until the pastry is well browned. Serve immediately with freshly cooked vegetables in season.

# chicken and *onion pot roast*

A celebration of onions in a simple dish. I love pot roasts, which are a meal in

themselves, needing no other accompaniment than crusty bread.

**Preparation time: 25 minutes Cooking time: about 1³/₄ hours**

*Serves 4 to 6*

Cook the shallots in the oil in a heavy-based pan that is just large enough to take the chicken. Cook until browned on all sides, then scoop them from the pan with a slotted spoon and set aside.

Add the chicken, brown quickly on all sides, then leave it in the pan, breast-side down. Press the quartered onions down the sides of the pan around it, with the thyme and lemon rind.

Season the chicken well, then add the stock with the saffron strands mixed in well. Bring to a boil and cover with a tight-fitting lid. Reduce the heat and simmer very gently for 45 minutes.

Turn the chicken over, then nestle it back down amongst the onions. Add the shallots and cook slowly, covered, for a further 45 minutes, or until the chicken is done – the juices should run clear from the thigh when pierced with a skewer.

Carefully draining any juices from the body cavity, transfer the chicken to a warm plate and leave it to rest for 10 minutes.

Add the spring onions to the sauce and boil briefly to reduce the quantity of liquid. Season to taste.

Carve the chicken and serve with the onions and juices spooned over.

12 to 15 shallots, peeled but
  left whole
3 Tbsp olive oil
1 oven-ready chicken, about
  1.8 kg (4 lb)
2 large yellow onions and
  2 red onions, quartered
3 to 4 large thyme sprigs
4 large strips pared lemon rind
Salt and black pepper
250 mL (9 fl oz) chicken or
  vegetable stock
A few strands of saffron
8 spring onions, finely chopped

# lamb and *onion curry*

*Serves 6*

1 kg (2¹/₄ lb) onions, chopped

4 cm (1¹/₂ in) piece fresh root
   ginger, peeled and chopped

6 garlic cloves

1 Tbsp black peppercorns

2 Tbsp coriander seeds

1 Tbsp cumin seeds

1 tsp green cardamom pods or
   ¹/₂ tsp ground cardamom

2 Tbsp oil

1 kg (2¹/₄ lb) lean boneless
   lamb, cut into 4 cm (1¹/₂ in)
   cubes

2 tsp ground turmeric

3 dried red chillies

2 tsp salt

1 Tbsp vinegar of your choice

250 mL (9 fl oz) water

1 tsp garam masala

5 Tbsp coconut cream

150 mL (5 fl oz) double cream

Fresh coriander to garnish

Onions are an essential part of a curry – I think they are best puréed to make

a base for a rich, spicy sauce.

**Preparation time: 30 minutes Cooking time: 1¹/₂ hours**

Purée the onions, ginger, and garlic to a smooth paste in a food processor.

Heat a large pan then add the peppercorns, coriander seeds, cumin seeds and cardamom and cook for about 30 seconds until fragrant. Turn out of the pan into a mortar or a small bowl and allow to cool slightly.

Heat the oil in the pan, then add the lamb and cook until coloured all over – it does not need to be really brown. Add the onion purée and cook for 4 to 5 minutes.

Crush the spices with a pestle or the end of a rolling pin then add them to the lamb with the turmeric and dried chillies. Cook for a further 2 to 3 minutes.

Stir in the salt, vinegar and water, then bring to a gentle boil. Cover the pan and simmer gently for 1 hour, until the lamb is just tender.

Stir in the garam masala, coconut cream and cream and continue cooking, uncovered, for 30 minutes, until the lamb is meltingly soft and the sauce has thickened.

Season to taste and serve garnished with fresh coriander.

*lamb and onion curry*

# mussels with *onions, apple and cider*

*Serves 2 as a main course or 4 as a starter*

1 kg (2¼ lb) mussels

1 large onion, finely chopped or sliced

1 tsp ground mace

2 Tbsp olive oil

1 garlic clove, minced

1 tart green apple, such as Granny Smith, cored and finely chopped

250 mL (9 fl oz) cider

2 bay leaves

Black pepper, sugar and lemon juice to taste

2 Tbsp crème fraîche or soured cream

2 Tbsp chopped fresh parsley

I have always loved mussels – there are so many ways of cooking them.

This is my latest idea – the flavour is intense.

Preparation time: 15 minutes Cooking time: 10–12 minutes

Wash and scrub the mussels, discarding any which are damaged or which do not close when tapped sharply. Pull off any beards.

Cook the onion with the mace in the oil in a large pan until softened, then add the garlic and apple. Add the cider and bay leaves. Bring to a rapid boil.

Stir in the mussels, cover the pan and cook over a very high heat for about 3 minutes, shaking the pan occasionally, until the mussels have all opened. Discard any that have failed to do so. Spoon the mussels into warmed serving bowls while the pan is still on the heat – this starts the sauce reducing quickly.

Continue to boil the liquor quickly until reduced by about half, then remove from the heat and season with pepper, sugar and a squeeze of lemon juice. Discard the bay leaves, then whisk in the crème fraîche or soured cream and parsley.

Spoon the sauce over the mussels and serve immediately, with plenty of crusty bread to mop up the sauce.

# liver *and onions*

*Serves 4*

2 large onions, sliced but not too finely

600 g (1¼ lb) liver, thinly sliced

3 Tbsp olive oil

Salt and black pepper

2 Tbsp plain flour

1 tsp mustard powder

250 mL (9 fl oz) onion or vegetable stock

Chopped fresh parsley to garnish

I love liver, but always choose lamb's or calf's liver which are milder than pig's. The best way to cook it is with lots of caramelized onions.

Preparation time: 10 minutes Cooking time: 15 minutes

Cook the onions in the olive oil in a large frying pan for 4 to 5 minutes while preparing the liver. Season the liver.

Mix the flour and mustard powder together and generously dust the liver with it. Move the onions to one side in the pan, add the liver and fry for 3 to 4 minutes on a medium-high heat on each side. Do not overcook, or the liver will be tough.

Transfer the liver to warmed plates, then add the stock to the pan. Bring to the boil, stirring all the time, and season the gravy to taste. Add a little more stock if you like a thinner sauce. Pour the onion gravy over the liver and garnish with plenty of chopped parsley before serving.

*mussels with onions, apple and cider*

# italian braised beef *with onion and aubergine*

*Serves 4*

2 Tbsp plain flour

Salt and black pepper

1 tsp mild chilli powder

4 beef shanks, each weighing
about 175 g (6 oz)

5 Tbsp olive oil

2 large garlic cloves, sliced

2 Tbsp chopped fresh oregano

400 g (14 oz) can chopped
tomatoes

450 mL (16 fl oz) beef or
vegetable stock

2 medium aubergines, cut into
chunks about 5 cm (2 in)

1 large onion, cut into 6

1 red onion, cut into 6

1 red pepper, seeded and diced

1 garlic clove, finely chopped

8 slices pancetta or very thin
bacon rashers

Chopped fresh parsley to
garnish

A perfect dinner or supper party dish – the meat cooks slowly in the oven
until very tender. Serve with a simple vegetable stir-fry.

Preparation time: 15 minutes Cooking time: about 3½ hours

Preheat the oven to 170°C/325°F/Gas Mark 3. Mix together the flour, seasonings and
chilli powder on a plate. Trim the beef and turn it in the flour.

Heat 3 tablespoons of the oil in an ovenproof casserole, add the beef and brown
well on both sides. Stir in the garlic, oregano and tomatoes and just enough stock
to cover the meat. Bring to the boil then cover the pan and transfer to the oven for
3 hours, or until the beef is meltingly tender.

Heat the remaining oil in a hot wok, add the aubergine and cook quickly to brown.
Add the onion and cook for a further 3 minutes, then add the pepper and garlic and
stir-fry for 2 minutes.

Remove the beef from the tomato sauce, transfer to a plate, cover with foil and
keep warm. Add the vegetables to the tomato sauce and simmer, uncovered, for about
10 minutes, until the vegetables are just done and the sauce is well reduced.

Dry-fry the pancetta or bacon in the wok until crisp.

To serve, make a mound of vegetables in the centre of four warmed serving plates
and top each with a piece of beef. Spoon the sauce over and around the plate, then
garnish each helping with a little of the crisp pancetta or bacon and some chopped
parsley. Serve immediately.

# veal with onion *and tuna mayonnaise*

This is an elegant summer dish – perfect for relaxed entertaining because it has to be prepared a day in advance. Adding onion to the veal as it cooks and shallot to the mayonnaise lifts the flavour enormously.

**Preparation time: 30 minutes Cooking time: 2 hours, plus overnight chilling**

Trim the joint and open it out on a chopping board. Pound the anchovies, one of the chopped onions and capers together, or process to a chunky paste with a hand blender. Add a little pepper, then smear the paste over the veal. Roll up the joint, tie it securely, and place in a pan just large enough to hold it.

Press the remaining chopped onions around the sides of the joint, add the peppercorns and parsley then pour in the stock, adding just enough to cover the veal.

Bring to the boil, then half cover the pan and simmer very slowly for 2 hours, until the veal is just tender. Leave to cool in the stock.

Chill the veal well (if possible, I like to leave it overnight in the stock in the fridge). Slice to serve.

To make the mayonnaise, whip the tuna, the remaining anchovies and the shallot with the tomato purée, lemon juice and mayonnaise. Season to taste – you will probably only need pepper. Stir in the chopped parsley, then serve spooned over the veal slices.

*Serves 6 to 8*

1.2-kg (2¼-lb) joint boneless veal
6 anchovy fillets, chopped
3 onions, finely chopped
2 Tbsp capers, roughly chopped
Salt and black pepper
6 black peppercorns
4 large sprigs parsley
500 mL (18 fl oz) chicken or
  vegetable stock

MAYONNAISE
100 g (3½ oz) canned tuna,
  drained
6 anchovy fillets
1 shallot, finely chopped
1 Tbsp tomato purée
Juice of 1 lemon
250 mL (9 fl oz) mayonnaise
2 Tbsp fresh chopped flat leaf
  parsley

*meat & fish*

# pork with *caramelized onions and apples*

*Serves 4*

1 Tbsp butter

4 Tbsp olive oil

2 apples, each cut into 4 thick
slices

1 Tbsp sugar

1 sweet and 1 red onion,
thickly sliced

500 g (1 lb) pork tenderloin,
trimmed and cut into 1 cm
('/2 in) slices

1 Tbsp plain flour

Salt and black pepper

1 Tbsp crushed coriander seeds

150 mL (5 fl oz) vegetable
stock

2 bay leaves

150 mL (5 fl oz) double cream

Snipped fresh chives to garnish

This is a classic combination of flavours – one that has endured for years
simply because it is so good.

Preparation time: 15 minutes Cooking time: 15 minutes

Heat the butter and 2 tablespoons of the oil together in a large frying pan. Turn the
apple slices in the sugar, then fry them quickly on both sides until browned. Transfer
to a plate and reserve for garnish.

Add the onions to the juices in the frying pan and toss them well – they will
quickly start to brown and caramelize. Cook over a moderate heat for about
5 minutes, stirring frequently. Turn on to a plate.

Heat the remaining oil in the pan. Dust the pork in the flour, seasonings and
coriander, then brown it quickly on both sides. Add the stock and bay leaves, bring to
the boil then simmer for 5 minutes.

Return the onions to the frying pan with the cream and simmer for a further
5 minutes.

Season to taste with extra salt and pepper then serve garnished with the reserved
apple rings and snipped chives.

# spiced pork with onions, *chillies and coconut*

*Serves 4*

2 Tbsp sunflower or
groundnut oil

1 boneless leg of pork,
weighing about 1 kg (2'/4 lb)

2 large onions, quartered

1 tsp ground turmeric

2 hot red chillies, finely chopped

2 tsp fresh tamarind paste
(optional)

3 to 4 lime leaves, finely
chopped or finely grated zest
of 2 limes

450 mL (16 fl oz) milk

3 Tbsp coconut cream

Salt and black pepper

A pleasantly spiced oven pot roast with modern, fusion flavours.
A great dinner party dish.

Preparation time: 20 minutes Cooking time: 2'/2 hours

Preheat the oven to 170°C/325°F/Gas Mark 3.

Heat the oil in an ovenproof casserole, then add the pork and brown quickly on all
sides. Transfer the meat to a plate.

Add the onions, spices and lime leaves or zest to the pan and cook until the onions
are lightly browned. Gradually add the milk, scraping up any bits from the base of the
pan, then bury the pork back in amongst the onions.

Bring just to the boil, cover and place in the oven for 2 to 2'/2 hours, until the
meat is tender. Remove the meat from the casserole and allow to stand for
10 minutes before carving.

Whisk the coconut cream into the spiced onions and milk, season and heat gently
until ready to serve. Carve the pork, and serve with the onion and coconut sauce
spooned over – broccoli and mashed potatoes or rice are good with this.

*pork with caramelized onions and apples*

# aubergine, red onion *and minced beef bake*

*Serves 4*

450 g (1 lb) lean minced beef

2 tsp ground cumin

1 Tbsp ground coriander

1 tsp ground ginger

400 g (14 oz) can chopped
  tomatoes

1 Tbsp chopped fresh oregano

2 bay leaves

Salt and black pepper

2 medium aubergines, sliced

150 mL (5 fl oz) olive oil

1 large red onion, cut into
  thin rings

40 g (1½ oz) flaked almonds

1 large egg, beaten

250 mL (9 fl oz) milk

The mild red onion flavour is offset by the spicy minced beef filling – use lamb if you prefer. You can scatter grated cheese over the top and brown the dish instead of using almonds and the egg custard.

**Preparation time: 40 minutes Cooking time: 1 hour**

Preheat the oven to 200°C/400°F/Gas Mark 6.

Cook the beef in a non-stick saucepan over a high heat until the fat and juices start to run. Add the spices and continue to cook until the meat is well browned.

Add the tomatoes, oregano, bay leaves and some seasoning, then leave to simmer for about 20 minutes. Season again to taste.

Fry the aubergine slices in two batches in a large frying pan. They will absorb all the oil and try to demand more, but don't give in! Fry until lightly browned.

Arrange half the aubergine slices in the base of a buttered ovenproof dish, then pour on the beef. Cover with the remaining aubergine, pressing them down well into the browned beef.

Separate the onion into rings and arrange them over the aubergine. Cover with foil then bake in the preheated oven for 40 minutes.

Lower the oven temperature to 170°C/325°F/Gas Mark 3. Remove the bake from the oven, take off the foil and scatter the almonds over the onions.

Beat the egg with the milk, add a little seasoning then pour the mixture over the almonds. Return to the oven for a further 15 to 20 minutes, until the topping is set. Serve hot with freshly cooked vegetables in season.

# duck breasts with *shallots and sherry*

This is a really simple recipe to prepare and cook,

but it is impressive – and delicious.

*Serves 4*

2 banana or large shallots,
  finely chopped
4 duck breast fillets
Coarse sea salt
4 Tbsp sherry vinegar
4 Tbsp medium sherry

**Preparation time: 5 minutes Cooking time: 40 minutes**

Preheat the oven to 200°C/400°F/Gas Mark 6.

Place the shallots in the base of a small roasting pan, then set the duck breasts, fat side uppermost, on a rack over them. Rub the breasts generously with coarse salt, then roast them in the hot oven for 30 to 35 minutes, until the juices run clear. Remove the rack and keep the duck warm for at least 5 minutes before carving.

Spoon off all but 2 tablespoons of the fat – keep it for roasting potatoes. Add the sherry vinegar to the pan and heat it gently on the stove, scraping up any bits from the base.

Stir in the sherry, bring to the boil then season to taste.

Slice the duck breasts and serve with the sauce spooned over.

# onion–studded lamb *with spring onion mash*

Shoulder of lamb is by far my favourite roasting cut because the meat

is so sweet and succulent. Instead of larding the joint with garlic or rosemary

I like to use sliced shallots, which give a really good onion flavour.

Serve with Champ (spring onion mash) – page 125.

*Serves 6*

2 banana shallots or 4 to 5
  button shallots, half finely
  chopped and half slivered
3 large sprigs of thyme
1 large shoulder of lamb,
  weighing about 2.3 kg (5 lb)
Salt and black pepper
1 Tbsp flour
About 450 mL (16 fl oz)
  vegetable stock

**Preparation time: 15 minutes Cooking time: about 2 hours, depending on size of joint**

Preheat the oven to 200°C/400°F/Gas Mark 6. Arrange the chopped shallots in the base of a roasting pan and top with the thyme.

Pierce the lamb repeatedly with the tip of a sharp knife, then insert slivers of the shallot. The more patience you have to persist with this, the better the flavour will be.

Place the lamb on top of the shallots in the roasting pan, season generously then rub the seasonings into the fat.

Roast the lamb for 1½ to 1¾ hours, then allow to stand for 15 minutes before carving. Discard the thyme, but use the chopped shallots and pan juices to make gravy by adding the flour and stirring over a low heat until bubbling. Gradually add in the stock, then bring to the boil, stirring all the time. Season to taste, simmer for 1 to 2 minutes, then serve with the sliced lamb and Champ.

# venison and *onion pie*

*Serves 6 to 8*

750 g (1³/₄ lb) stewing venison,
or boneless pork loin, diced

450 g (1 lb) onions, chopped

Salt and black pepper

6 juniper berries, crushed

3 Tbsp red wine

2 Tbsp olive oil

1 egg, beaten

1 tsp gelatin

150 mL (5 fl oz) boiling
vegetable stock

PASTRY

225 g (8 oz) plain flour

1 tsp salt

175 g (6 oz) lard

125 mL (4 fl oz) water and
milk, mixed

Venison makes an ideal filling for this traditional raised pie as it hardly shrinks at all during cooking. A generous amount of onion in the pie adds lots of flavour and keeps the meat moist.

**Preparation time: 45 minutes Cooking time: 1¹/₂–1³/₄ hours**

Prepare the pastry. Place the flour and salt in a bowl and make a well in the centre. Chop the lard, add it to the liquids, then heat until melted. Bring to a rolling boil, then pour into the flour and mix immediately into a soft, manageable dough. Knead until smooth on a lightly floured surface, then cover and leave to cool slightly.

Preheat the oven to 220°C/425°F/Gas Mark 7. Process the venison and onions in a food processor or meat grinder until finely chopped, then season well. Add the juniper berries and moisten the meat with the wine and oil.

Roll out two-thirds of the pastry and use to line an 20 cm (8 in) deep springform pan. Pack the meat into the pie, then roll out the remaining pastry to make a lid. Moisten the edges of the pastry, then seal the top and sides together, pressing the edge into a decorative crust. Make a small slit in the centre of the lid and use any pastry trimmings to make decorative leaves.

Brush the top of the pie with beaten egg, then bake in the hot oven for 15 minutes. Lower the temperature to 180°C/350°F/Gas Mark 4 and cook for a further 1 hour.

Carefully loosen and remove the sides of the pan trying not to break the pastry, then brush all the pastry again with beaten egg. Continue to cook for a further 20 to 30 minutes, brushing with egg once or twice more until the pastry is a dark, golden brown. Remove the pie from the oven and leave to cool slightly.

Dissolve the gelatin in the hot stock then pour it carefully into the pie – you will probably only get a small amount in as the meat hardly shrinks at all during cooking. Leave the pie until cold, then chill it for 2 to 3 hours before slicing. Serve cold, with some strong pickles and a green salad.

*venison and onion pie*

# chinese salmon *with spring onions and ginger*

*Serves 4 to 6*

1 small whole salmon or a large
  piece of salmon, weighing
  about 1.2 kg (2³/₄ lb)
8 spring onions, trimmed and
  finely sliced
5 cm (2 in) piece fresh root
  ginger, peeled and finely
  chopped
1 to 2 red chillies, seeded and
  chopped fine
Light soy sauce
4 Tbsp sesame oil

The Chinese usually serve a whole fish at their New Year's banquets. I like this at any time of the year – the spicing adds extra flavour to the salmon.

**Preparation time: 15 minutes Cooking time: 35 minutes**

Preheat the oven to 220°C/425°F/Gas Mark 7. Lightly oil a large sheet of heavy foil, big enough to enclose the salmon, and place it on a lipped baking sheet.

Trim the salmon and slash the flesh deeply three times on each side – this helps the fish to cook more quickly. Place the fish on the foil and insert half the spring onions, all the ginger and the chillies into the cavity – press a little of the onion mixture into the slits as well, if you like. Shake just a little soy sauce over the fish, then wrap it loosely in the foil. Bake in the hot oven for about 30 minutes, until the flesh offers no resistance when pierced with the tip of a sharp knife. Take care not to overcook the salmon or it will be dry.

Divide the salmon into portions and scatter the remaining spring onions among them. Meanwhile, heat the sesame oil in a small pan, then pour it over the salmon just before serving.

# home-made beef burgers *with spring onions*

*Serves 4*

450 g (1 lb) minced beef
115 g (4 oz) coarsely grated
  mozzarella cheese
4 spring onions, trimmed and
  very finely chopped
Salt and black pepper
1 egg yolk
Rolls or baps and salad to serve

Home-made beef burgers are a real treat. Adding onion gives them loads of flavour, but make sure it is finely chopped or the burgers may fall apart during cooking.

**Preparation time: 15 minutes Cooking time: 12 minutes**

Mix all the ingredients together in a bowl, binding them with the egg yolk. Shape into four burgers – wetting your hands makes them easier to handle.

Heat a ridged grill pan until hot. Add the burgers and cook over a moderate heat for 4 to 5 minutes on each side. No additional oil should be necessary – just rely on the fat in the meat. Serve hot in baps or burger rolls with salad.

*chinese salmon with spring onions and ginger*

# traditional steak and *onion pudding*

*Serves 6 to 8*

2 large onions, very thinly
   sliced

750 g (1³/₄ lb) best braising
   steak, cut into 2 cm (³/₄ in)
   cubes

140 g (5 oz) mushrooms,
   thickly sliced

Salt and black pepper

450 g (1 lb) plain flour

1 Tbsp baking powder

1 tsp salt

550 g (1¹/₄ lb) lard or margarine

Cold water to mix

150 mL (5 fl oz) beer

A variation of the classic English meat pudding – a good helping of onions provides a tasty alternative to the traditional pairing of steak and kidney.

**Preparation time: 40 minutes Cooking time: 4–5 hours**

Half-fill the base of a steamer with water and bring to the boil. Lightly butter a 2 litre (3¹/₂ pints) pudding dish.

Mix together the onions, steak, mushrooms and seasoning.

Sift the flour and baking powder together into a large bowl, add the salt and stir in the lard or margarine. Mix to a soft manageable dough with cold water, then knead lightly on a floured surface.

Roll the pastry out into a large circle, about twice the diameter of the pudding dish rim. Cut away a segment (about one-third) of the dough, then press the remainder into the basin to line the base and sides, sealing any joins with a little water.

Pack the meat into the pudding, then pour in the beer. Roll out the remaining pastry to form a lid and use it to cover the pudding, damping and sealing the edges together. Make a small slit in the lid. It is no problem if the pudding does not completely fill the basin.

Cover with greased greaseproof paper and foil, making a fold in the covers to allow for the pastry to rise. Tie securely, to keep the cover on and the steam out.

Steam the pudding over boiling water for 4 to 5 hours – the longer the better. Top up the water as required. Add a little boiling stock or vegetable water to the meat when serving – cut away the first portion of pastry from the lid, then pour the extra liquid into the pudding. Serve with a selection of freshly cooked vegetables.

# braised pheasant *with onions and celery*

Braised in a sauce that is sweet, sour and fruity, the pheasant may be cooked quickly to keep the vegetables crisp, or slowly to provide a more meltingly tender result. Time and preference will dictate.

**Preparation time: 45 minutes Cooking time: 1 hour, or 1 1/2–1 3/4 hours**

Preheat the oven to 200°C/400°F/Gas Mark 6. Dust the pheasants generously with the flour, season then brown the portions well in the oil in a large frying pan.

Meanwhile, place the prepared vegetables and cranberries in a casserole dish that will take the pheasants in one layer, and bury the thyme in the vegetables. Nestle the pheasants into the vegetables.

Add all the remaining ingredients to the pan and bring to the boil. Pour over the pheasants, then cover with a lid or foil.

Cook in the hot oven for 10 minutes, then lower the temperature to 190°C/375°F/ Gas Mark 5 for 45 to 50 minutes, or to 170°C/325°F/Gas Mark 3 for 1 1/2 to 1 3/4 hours. The pheasant is cooked if the juices run clear when the thigh is pierced with the tip of a sharp knife.

Season the sauce to taste, then serve the pheasant on a bed of the vegetables with the juices spooned over and garnished with celery leaves.

*Serves 4*

2 hen pheasants, cut
   lengthways in half
2 Tbsp plain flour
Salt and black pepper
4 Tbsp olive oil
6 sticks celery, trimmed and cut
   into 5 cm (2 in) pieces
   (reserve the leaves to garnish)
2 large onions, cut into 6
2 large carrots, cut into 2.5 cm
   (1 in) pieces
50 g (1 3/4 oz) dried cranberries
4–5 large thyme sprigs
Juice of 1 lemon
3 Tbsp red wine vinegar
4 Tbsp clear honey
250 mL (9 fl oz) chicken or
   vegetable stock

# pasta with onions, *clams and tomato*

*Serves 2*

1 onion, finely chopped

1 Tbsp olive oil

150 mL (5 fl oz) fish stock, dry
white wine or a mixture of
both

1 garlic clove, minced

2 Tbsp chopped fresh mixed
herbs for fish (dill, chervil,
flat leaf parsley)

450 g (1 lb) clams, rinsed and
scrubbed if necessary

200 g (7 oz) pasta, freshly
cooked

Salt and black pepper

2 tomatoes, seeded and chopped

Chopped fresh parsley to
garnish

A perfect supper dish – plenty of flavour, interesting textures,

colourful to look at and quick to prepare.

**Preparation time: 10 minutes Cooking time: 12-15 minutes**

Cook the onion slowly in the oil until soft and translucent. Add the liquid and bring
to a rapid boil, then add the garlic, herbs and clams. Cover and cook for 3 to 4
minutes, until the clams have just opened. Discard any clams that do not open. Shake
the pan from time to time.

Drain the pasta, then add the clams and onions to the pasta along with a knob of
butter and some seasoning. Toss together.

Meanwhile, boil the onion and clam juices with the chopped tomatoes for
2 minutes then pour over the pasta. Mix well and serve immediately, garnished with
chopped parsley.

# sausages and onions *with beer gravy*

*Serves 2*

2 Tbsp olive oil

6 thick sausages

2 large onions, thinly sliced

1 Tbsp plain flour

150 mL (5 fl oz) beer

150 mL (5 fl oz) onion or
vegetable stock or water

Salt and black pepper

Mashed potatoes to serve

A new twist on a traditional English favourite. Accompanied by a helping of

mashed potatoes is a great way to serve these sausages.

**Preparation time: 10 minutes Cooking time: 35 minutes**

Heat the oil in a large frying pan then add the sausages and brown them quickly on
all sides to seal them.

Stir in the onions, toss in the hot oil, then lower the heat to medium and cook for
20 minutes, turning the sausages occasionally.

Remove the sausages from the frying pan and keep them warm. Scatter the flour
over the onions, then stir it in over the heat breaking up any lumps that form.
Gradually add the beer and stock, then bring the gravy to the boil, stirring continuously.

Season to taste. I like to serve this with a mound of mashed potatoes, the sausages
resting against it, then the gravy spooned around the plate and vegetables scattered
among the onions.

*pasta with onions, clams and tomato*

# teriyaki venison with *onion and sour cherries*

4 venison steaks, about
175 g (6 oz) each
Salt and black pepper
Generous pinch of dried
crushed chillies
2 Tbsp groundnut oil
175 mL (6 fl oz) plus 3 Tbsp
bottled teriyaki marinade
50 g (1¾ oz) dried sour
cherries
150 mL (5 fl oz) vegetable or
chicken stock
1 small sweet onion, finely
chopped
1 Tbsp groundnut oil
Black pepper and sugar to taste
Fresh coriander to garnish

The sweetness of the onion combines well with the salty teriyaki marinade

and flavoursome sour cherries in this delicious dinner party dish.

If dried cherries are unavailable, substitute dried cranberries.

**Preparation time: 25 minutes, plus marinating time Cooking time: 12–15 minutes**

Season the steaks lightly, and place them in a strong, resealable plastic bag. Add the chillies, oil and 3 tablespoons of the teriyaki marinade, then expel the air from the bag and seal it firmly. Rub the marinade thoroughly into the meat, then leave in the fridge for at least 2 hours.

Soak the cherries in the stock while the venison is marinating.

Carefully remove the steaks from the bag and reserve the marinade. Pat the meat dry on kitchen paper. Heat a ridged grill pan, add the steaks and cook for 3 to 4 minutes on each side, depending on thickness and how rare you like your meat.

Meanwhile, cook the onion in the oil in a small pan until soft, then add the remaining bottled teriyaki, the cherries and some of their soaking broth and the reserved marinade. Bring to the boil then simmer for 5 minutes. Season to taste and add a little more stock if necessary.

Serve the steaks sliced with the sauce spooned over, garnished with coriander. This is great served with Champ (page 125).

*teriyaki venison with onion and sour cherries*

# spanish–style cod *with onion and peppers*

*Serves 4*

450 g (1 lb) cod fillet or similar
   white fish, such as haddock,
   skinned
3 Tbsp olive oil
1 large red onion, finely sliced
85 g (3 oz) button mushrooms,
   sliced
1 red and 1 green pepper,
   seeded and sliced
Salt and white pepper
125 mL (4 fl oz) white wine
   vinegar
125 mL (4 fl oz) water
1 Tbsp sugar

Onions give lots of flavour to this traditional dish of lightly

cooked cod – a great summer dish.

**Preparation time: 15 minutes Cooking time: 15 minutes, plus 24 hours chilling time**

Cut the fish into bite-size pieces. Heat 2 tablespoons of the oil in a large frying pan and fry the fish until just done, then transfer it to a glass or ceramic dish.

Heat the remaining oil in the frying pan, add the onion and cook until soft but not browned. Stir in the mushrooms and peppers and cook for a further 1 to 2 minutes – the vegetables should remain crisp.

Spoon the vegetables over the fish and season lightly with salt and pepper.

Pour the vinegar and water into the frying pan and bring to the boil. Add the sugar, stir until dissolved, then pour over the fish and vegetables. Allow to cool then cover and refrigerate for 24 hours. Serve with crusty olive bread.

spanish-style cod with onion and peppers

# chicken, onion *and beansprout risotto*

*Serves 4*

2 large onions, finely sliced

2 Tbsp olive oil

2 chicken breast fillets, sliced

1 red pepper, seeded and sliced

300 g (10½ oz) cracked wheat

500 mL (18 fl oz) vegetable or
  chicken stock

3 Tbsp tamari or soy sauce

2 handfuls beansprouts

115 g (4 oz) dry-roasted,
  unsalted peanuts

Salt and black pepper

Chopped fresh parsley to
  garnish

I love risottos made with cracked wheat – they have more crunch than those made with rice. Here the onions and chicken really star for flavour, along with the peanuts.

Preparation time: 15 minutes Cooking time: 25 minutes

Cook the onions in the oil in a large frying pan until soft and just starting to brown; add the chicken and stir-fry until it is white all over.

Add the pepper and cracked wheat, and toss them in the pan juices, then add the stock. Season with the tamari or soy sauce, bring to the boil and simmer gently for 15 minutes, until most of the stock has been absorbed.

Add the beansprouts and peanuts. Season with salt and pepper if necessary, then continue cooking for a further 1 to 2 minutes to heat everything through.

Garnish with plenty of chopped parsley and serve with a side salad.

# vegetable main courses

*Green, red and golden onions are joined by the sweet white varieties in this choice of vegetable main dishes. Bake onions into pies, force them into ravioli or chop them into baked potatoes. Onions are essential for flavour-packed vegetable dishes.*

# cheese and onion *stuffed jacket potatoes*

*Serves 2*

2 large baking potatoes,
  weighing about 225 g (8 oz)
  each
2 red onions, halved
Olive oil
115 g (4 oz) Cheddar cheese,
  grated
Salt and black pepper
1 Tbsp butter or 1–2 Tbsp milk

Jacket potatoes are really special when the centres are scooped out,

mashed and seasoned – it's worth the extra effort!

Preparation time: 10 minutes Cooking time: 1½ hours

Preheat the oven to 200°C/400°F/Gas Mark 6. Scrub and score the potatoes, then place them in a small roasting pan with the onions. Drizzle the onions with olive oil then bake for 1 hour, or until the potatoes are done.

Slice the potatoes in half and scoop the soft centres out into a food processor. Add the baked onion, most of the cheese, seasonings and butter or milk and process until smooth in consistency.

Pile the filling back into the potatoes, top with the remaining cheese, and return to the oven for 10 to 15 minutes, or brown lightly under a hot grill.

# baked stuffed *onions*

*Serves 4*

4 large onions
85 g (3 oz) bulghur wheat
Salt and black pepper
125 mL (4 fl oz) boiling
  vegetable stock
1 Tbsp butter

Baked onions make a marvellously comforting food when you are

feeling under the weather. I have kept the filling simple,

so this is an ideal dish for delicate days.

Preparation time: 40 minutes Cooking time: 20 minutes

Preheat the oven to 200°C/400°F/Gas Mark 6. Peel the onions but leave their roots intact. Bring them to the boil in a pan of water and simmer for 15 to 20 minutes, until just tender.

Meanwhile, measure the bulghur wheat into a jug, transfer it to a bowl and add the same volume of water. Allow to stand until required.

Take the onions out of the pan and run them under cold water until cool enough to handle. Carefully cut around the tops with a very sharp knife, then scoop out the pulp with a teaspoon, leaving a secure shell. The root helps the onions to keep their shape while you are doing this.

Chop the onion pieces. Drain the bulghur wheat, then mix it with the chopped onion and a little seasoning. Pack the mixture back into the onions, and place them in a small, buttered ovenproof pan.

Add the boiling stock, top each onion with a little butter then bake them in the oven, uncovered, for 15 to 20 minutes until golden brown. Spoon a little of the stock over the onions once or twice during cooking.

*cheese and onion stuffed jacket potatoes*

# onion ravioli *with walnut and sorrel sauce*

*Serves 2*

2 large onions
4 Tbsp olive oil
1 garlic clove, finely chopped
Large pinch of ground mace
Salt and black pepper
12 sheets fresh no-precook
    lasagne
55 g (2 oz) chopped walnuts
115 g (4 oz) unsalted butter
1–2 Tbsp shredded sorrel

This is a rich and delicious pasta dish. Serve it as a main course with a simple side salad, or divide into smaller portions and serve as a starter.

**Preparation time: 30 minutes Cooking time: 10 minutes**

Chop one and a half of the onions, then cook them in the olive oil with the garlic and mace until soft and golden brown – about 10 minutes over a moderate heat. Add salt and pepper then allow to cool.

Dampen the edges and crossways along the middle of each sheet of lasagne, one at a time. Place about 1 teaspoon of onions on one end of each sheet, then fold the lasagne over in half and seal the edges to make a ravioli pouch. Leave on a damp dish towel until ready to cook.

Slice the remaining onion and cook it in the pan until golden with any remaining onion filling. Once browned, add the chopped walnuts and the butter. Heat until the butter has melted then keep warm.

Bring a large pan of salted water to the boil. Add the ravioli and cook gently for 3 to 4 minutes, then drain and add to the butter sauce with the shredded sorrel. Season to taste and serve.

# onion *moussaka*

*Serves 4*

2 large onions, chopped
2 Tbsp olive oil
450 g (1 lb) minced tofu or
    other meat substitute
150 mL (5 fl oz) red wine
400 g (14 oz) can chopped
    tomatoes
2 Tbsp chopped fresh oregano
Salt and black pepper
1 Tbsp tomato purée
2 large aubergines, sliced
Olive oil
225 g (8 oz) ricotta cheese
150 mL (5 fl oz) natural
    yoghurt
125 g (4½ oz) soft goat's
    cheese with garlic and herbs

A vegetarian moussaka which marries the rich flavours of aubergine and onion.

**Preparation time: 45 minutes Cooking time: 40 minutes**

Cook the onions in the oil in a covered pan until soft, then remove the lid and stir in the minced tofu or other meat substitute. Cook quickly for 2 to 3 minutes, then add the wine and cook until it has reduced by half. Add the tomatoes, oregano, seasonings and tomato purée then simmer gently for 30 to 40 minutes, until rich and thick.

Preheat the oven to 220°C/425°F/Gas Mark 7. Fry the aubergine slices in olive oil, a few at a time, until browned. Drain on kitchen paper and set aside until required.

Layer the onion sauce and aubergine slices in a buttered, ovenproof pan, finishing with a layer of aubergine. Blend the remaining ingredients together into a sauce, add salt and pepper to taste and spoon the mixture over the aubergine. Bake in the preheated oven for 25 to 30 minutes, until lightly browned. Serve immediately with a tossed green salad.

*onion ravioli with walnut and sorrel sauce*

# cheese and *onion fondue*

*Serves 4*

2 shallots

2 mild red chillies, seeded

300 mL (10 fl oz) cider

Juice of 1 lemon

450 g (1 lb) Swiss cheese,
  finely sliced or grated

Salt and black pepper

1 Tbsp cornflour

2–3 Tbsp Calvados (optional)

French bread and cucumber for
  dipping

Shallots work well in this recipe, providing lots of very good onion flavour without altering the consistency of the fondue too much. I purée the shallots, so they blend better into the melted cheese.

**Preparation time: 15 minutes Cooking time: 10 minutes**

Roughly chop the shallots and chillies, then blend them to a smooth purée, adding a little of the cider, if necessary.

Bring the cider and lemon juice to the boil, then add the cheese and seasonings. Stir constantly, over a low heat, until the cheese melts and starts to bubble.

Blend the cornflour with the Calvados or a little more cider, then stir it into the fondue. Cook for a further 3 to 4 minutes, until thickened.

Pour the fondue into a warmed dish and set over a table burner to keep warm and melted. Dip chunks of bread and cucumber into the pan to scoop up the cheese.

# lentil and *onion lasagne*

Lentils make a satisfying sauce for this vegetarian lasagne. For maximum convenience use lasagne that does not require precooking.

*Serves 6*

2 large onions, finely chopped

2 Tbsp olive oil

1 courgette, diced

1 green pepper, seeded and diced

175 g (6 oz) red lentils

400 g (14 oz) can chopped tomatoes

750 mL (1⅓ pints) vegetable stock

Salt and black pepper

2 Tbsp chopped fresh mixed herbs

8 sheets prepared no-precook lasagne, fresh or dried

225 g (8 oz) ricotta cheese

350 mL (12 fl oz) fromage frais or soured cream

115 g (4 oz) Cheddar cheese, grated

**Preparation time: 45 minutes Cooking time: 30-40 minutes**

Cook the onions in the oil until softened but not browned, then stir in the zucchini and bell pepper and cook for a further 2 minutes. Add the lentils and tomatoes and stir well. Add the broth and seasonings then bring the sauce to a boil. Simmer for 20 to 25 minutes, until the lentils are soft and the sauce has thickened.

Preheat the oven to 400°F (200°C). Place half the onion and lentil mixture in the bottom of a suitable buttered ovenproof pan and top with half the pasta. Repeat the layers. Mix the ricotta and fromage frais or sour cream together, then season with salt and pepper. Add half the cheese then spread the mixture over the lasagne, topping it with the remaining cheese.

Bake in the preheated oven for 30 to 40 minutes, until the topping is set and lightly browned.

# onion and *pepper pizza*

A quick pizza, made with a shopbought pizza base, for days when there is very little time to cook.

*Serves 2 to 3*

3 large onions, very finely sliced

3 Tbsp olive oil

1 prepared 25 cm (10 in) pizza base

1 red and 1 green pepper, seeded and cut into rings

Salt and black pepper

175 g (6 oz) mozzarella cheese, thinly sliced

12 black olives

**Preparation time: 15 minutes Cooking time: 10 minutes**

Preheat the oven to 220°C/425°F/Gas Mark 7.

Cook two-thirds of the onions in the oil for 5 minutes over high heat.

Place the pizza base on a baking sheet and top with the cooked onions. Arrange the peppers on top then finish with the remaining onion slices. Season well with salt and pepper.

Arrange the mozzarella over the vegetables and top with the olives. Drizzle with a little more olive oil if you wish.

Bake for 10 minutes, until the cheese is just beginning to melt, bubble and brown. Serve immediately with a green or tomato salad.

# cheese *and onion quiche*

*Serves 4*

6 to 8 spring onions, trimmed
  and finely chopped
1 Tbsp olive oil
½ tsp paprika
140 g (5 oz) plain flour, sieved
Salt and black pepper
6 Tbsp butter
115 g (4 oz) Cheddar cheese,
  grated
3 large eggs, beaten
425 mL (15 fl oz) milk

Properly cooked, the much-maligned quiche is delicious. The filling should be just set to wobbly perfection.

**Preparation time: 15 minutes Cooking time: 40 minutes**

Preheat the oven to 220°C/425°F/Gas Mark 7 and place a baking sheet in the oven to heat.

Cook the white part of the spring onions in the oil with the paprika until soft – about 4 minutes over a low heat. Allow to cool.

Mix the flour with a pinch of salt then rub into the butter until the mixture resembles fine breadcrumbs. Add just enough cold water to make a stiff dough then roll out and use to line a deep 20 cm (8 inch) flan tin, preferably with a loose base.

Mix the green part of the spring onions with the chopped white part and half the grated cheese then scatter over the base of the pastry. Beat the eggs into the milk, season lightly then pour the mixture over the onions. Scatter with the remaining cheese and sprinkle over a little more paprika.

Place the quiche on the hot baking sheet and cook for 10 minutes, then lower the oven temperature to 190°C/375°F/Gas Mark 5 and cook for a further 25 to 30 minutes, until the filling is just set.

Allow to stand for at least 10 minutes before cutting – quiche should be served either warm or cold.

# cheese *and onion pasties*

*Makes 4*

1 large potato, weighing about
  280 g (10 oz), finely diced
Salt and black pepper
One 375 g (13 oz) packet
  ready-rolled puff pastry
2 medium red onions, finely
  diced
175 g (6 oz) Cheddar cheese,
  diced
2 Tbsp snipped fresh chives
Milk to glaze

Appetizing, quick and easy – what more could you want from a simple supper dish?

**Preparation time: 25 minutes Cooking time: 20 minutes**

Preheat the oven to 220°C/425°F/Gas Mark 7. Bring the potato to the boil in a pan of salted water, then simmer for 1 minute. Drain and allow to cool slightly.

Cut out four 15 cm (6 in) circles from the pastry. Mix the potato with the remaining ingredients, then divide the filling among the four pastry circles.

Dampen the edges of the pastry with water, then gather the pastry together over the filling, pressing the edges firmly together to seal. Brush with milk.

Arrange the pasties on a baking sheet then bake in the hot oven for 15 to 20 minutes, until the pastry is golden. Serve warm or cold.

*cheese and onion quiche*

# cheese, rice *and onion loaf*

*Serves 6*

200 g (7 oz) brown rice

2 large onions, thickly sliced

4 Tbsp olive oil

1 red onion

2 courgettes

2 garlic cloves, minced

400 g (14 oz) wholemeal
  breadcrumbs

Salt and black pepper

1 large egg, beaten

115 g (4 oz) Cheddar cheese,
  grated

An excellent vegetarian loaf – a refreshing change from nut loaf or lentil bakes, and delicious served with a spiced fruit chutney.

**Preparation time: 45 minutes Cooking time: 45 minutes**

Cook the rice in a large pan of water – do not add salt as that will toughen the husk of the rice during cooking. Allow about 30 minutes for the rice to cook after it comes to the boil. Drain in a colander, then leave until required.

Preheat the oven to 190°C/375°F/Gas Mark 5. Cook the onion slices in 2 tablespoons of the olive oil until just softened. Leave until required.

Shred the red onion and courgettes on the coarse grating attachment of a food processor, then cook them in the remaining olive oil until just tender. Turn into a bowl and add the remaining ingredients, mixing thoroughly.

Butter a 900 g (2 lb) loaf pan and line the base with baking parchment. Arrange half the onion slices in a layer in the base of the pan, then top with half the rice mixture. Make a second layer of onion in the middle of the loaf and top with the remaining rice, packing it down firmly. Cover with a layer of buttered foil.

Bake the loaf in the preheated oven for 40 minutes. Remove the foil and ease the loaf away from the sides of the pan with a palette knife. Turn the loaf out on to a warmed plate and serve sliced.

# french bean *and onion frittata*

*Serves 3 to 4*

175 g (6 oz) fresh or frozen
  French beans

6 to 8 spring onions, trimmed
  and sliced

2 Tbsp olive oil

6 large eggs, beaten

2 Tbsp chopped flat leaf parsley

Salt and black pepper

40 g (1½ oz) Parmesan cheese,
  grated

Similar to a Spanish omelette but lighter as it contains no starchy potato, this is an elegant, summer supper dish.

**Preparation time: 10 minutes Cooking time: 20 minutes**

Cook the beans in boiling salted water for 4 minutes then drain.

Cook the spring onions in the oil in a 20 cm (8 in) non-stick frying pan for 2 to 3 minutes, then mix in the beans.

Beat the eggs with the parsley, seasonings and cheese. Pour the mixture into the frying pan, tossing the vegetables carefully to coat them in the eggs.

Cook over a very low heat for about 15 minutes, until the eggs are just set. If still runny on top when browned on the base, transfer the frying pan to a hot grill to finish cooking the top. Leave for 2 minutes, then cut into quarters to serve.

# blue cheese *and spring onion cheesecake*

This is really more of a souffléd quiche, delicious and different.

Serve with lots of green salad.

Serves 4 to 6

**PASTRY**
140 g (5 oz) plain flour
Pinch of salt
6 Tbsp butter

**FILLING**
225 g (8 oz) ricotta cheese
2 large eggs, separated
1 tsp instant dry yeast
8 spring onions, trimmed and
   finely chopped
115 g (4 oz) blue cheese,
   crumbled
Black pepper
Soured cream to serve

**Preparation time: 30 minutes Cooking time: 40 minutes**

Preheat the oven to 200°C/400°F/Gas Mark 6, and place a baking sheet in the oven. Prepare the pastry by mixing the flour and salt in a bowl, and then rubbing in the butter until the mixture resembles fine breadcrumbs. Mix to a firm dough with cold water, then roll out and line a deep 20 cm (8 in) pan, preferably springform. Chill until required.

Beat the ricotta with the egg yolks and yeast, then stir in the chopped spring onions, blue cheese and black pepper. Whisk the egg whites until stiff, then fold them into the mixture. Spoon the filling into the prepared pastry case.

Place the cheesecake in the hot oven and immediately reduce the heat to 190°C/375°F/Gas Mark 5 and bake for 35 to 40 minutes, until the filling is set and golden.

Cool the cheesecake for about 15 minutes then slice and serve warm, with a spoonful of soured cream.

# onion *filo pie*

*Serves 6*

4 sweet and 2 red onions,
   sliced

100 mL (3½ fl oz) groundnut oil

1 hot red chilli, seeded and
   finely chopped

5 to 6 lime leaves, shredded, or
   finely grated zest of 3 limes

1 stalk lemon grass, bruised
   and finely chopped

55 g (2 oz) flaked coconut

Salt

2 Tbsp soy sauce

10 to 14 sheets filo pastry,
   depending on size

I use a mixture of red and sweet onions to fill this light summer pie –

just serve with green and tomato salads for great outdoor food.

Do cook this in a tin and not a ceramic pan, or the base will never

begin to crisp. It is very rich, so serve small portions.

**Preparation time: 40 minutes Cooking time: 40 minutes**

Soften the onions in a large frying pan in 3 tablespoons of the oil, add the chilli, lime leaves or zest and lemon grass, and cook slowly for 15 to 20 minutes, until the onions are softened. Stir in the coconut, add salt to taste, then allow to cool slightly.

Preheat the oven to 200°C/400°F/Gas Mark 6. Blend the oil and soy sauce together. Arrange most of the filo sheets in a buttered, deep 20 cm (8 in) round pan, overlapping the sides of the pan and forming a pastry case at least three layers thick. Brush each sheet with oil and soy sauce to keep them moist.

Press the onion mixture into the lined pan, then cover with two more sheets of filo, folded in half. Turn the pastry edges in over the pie, score the top of the pastry with a sharp knife, then brush generously with the remaining oil and soy sauce.

Place the pie on a baking sheet and bake for about 30 minutes, until the pastry is crisp and deep golden brown.

Cool slightly before serving sliced with a stir-fry of mixed vegetables.

# onion *and saffron risotto*

The temptation with risotto is to add too many flavouring ingredients.

Resist at all costs! Just the onion and saffron are a perfect combination,

when garnished with the fried garlic.

**Preparation time: 10 minutes Cooking time: 30–40 minutes**

*Serves 4*

Set the vegetable stock to the boil, then heat the oil and butter together in a large frying pan, add the chopped onions and cook slowly for 6 to 8 minutes, until softened but not browned. Add the saffron to the boiling stock.

Stir the rice into the frying pan and coat it in the onion juices, then add about one-third of the stock. Simmer until absorbed, stirring from time to time, then add half the remaining stock. Continue until all the stock has been absorbed into the risotto, giving a moist, creamy consistency – add a little more stock if necessary.

Meanwhile, heat about 2.5 cm (1 in) of olive oil in a small pan, add the garlic slices and fry until golden brown. Drain on kitchen paper – keep the olive oil to add to mashed potatoes or to use for frying.

Season the risotto to taste and serve hot, garnished with the fried garlic.

1.5 L (2¾ pints) vegetable
  stock
2 Tbsp olive oil
1 Tbsp butter
1 large onion and 2 red onions,
  chopped
A few strands of saffron
280 g (10 oz) risotto rice
Olive oil to deep-fry
2 large garlic cloves, sliced
Salt and black pepper

# onion and *gorgonzola ciabatta pizza*

*Serves 2*

1 large onion, finely sliced

1 red onion, finely sliced

3 Tbsp olive oil

1 ready-to-bake ciabatta loaf

1 large garlic clove, finely
   chopped

6 to 8 anchovy fillets, chopped

Salt and black pepper

2 to 3 thyme sprigs

1 small red pepper, sliced

115 g (4 oz) Gorgonzola cheese,
   crumbled

Olive oil to drizzle (optional)

The Gorgonzola melts seductively over the onions drawing out the flavours of the Mediterranean. A crunchy, unusual pizza and a great alternative to tomatoes.

**Preparation time: 15 minutes Cooking time: 10 minutes**

Preheat the oven to 220°C/425°F/Gas Mark 7. Meanwhile, cook most of the onions in the oil over a moderate heat for 10 minutes, stirring occasionally.

Bake the ciabatta for 5 minutes. At the same time, add the garlic, anchovy, seasoning and thyme to the onions and continue cooking.

Split the baked ciabatta horizontally and spread the onion mixture over the two halves on a baking sheet. Top with the remaining onion and the pepper then finish with the cheese. Drizzle with a little olive oil if you wish.

Bake in the hot oven for a further 5 to 8 minutes, until the cheese has melted and is lightly browned, then serve immediately.

# spanish *onion omelette*

I first had Spanish omelette when my aunt had a Spanish au pair – we used to

love having Maria look after us and cook for us in the holidays.

**Preparation time: 15 minutes Cooking time: 12–15 minutes**

*Serves 2 to 3*

Heat the oil in an 20 cm (8 in) preferably non-stick frying pan. Add the potato and cook slowly for 4 to 5 minutes, stirring occasionally.

Add the onion and pepper and continue cooking for a further 6 to 8 minutes, until all the vegetables are tender. Season well.

Add the eggs and stir them through the vegetables. Cook slowly for about 10 minutes, until the eggs are set. If they are not cooked on top before the base is browned, finish the omelette off under a hot grill.

Allow to stand for a minute or two, then serve hot, cut into wedges and garnished with parsley.

2-3 Tbsp olive oil

1 large potato, finely diced

1 large Spanish onion, finely sliced

1 green pepper, finely sliced

Salt and black pepper

4 large eggs, beaten

flat leaf parsley to garnish

# onion *and sweet chestnut casserole*

*Serves 4*

12 small pickling onions
3 Tbsp olive oil
2 medium leeks, sliced
1 red and 1 yellow pepper,
   sliced
2 garlic cloves, sliced
2 Tbsp wholemeal flour
600 mL (1 pint) vegetable stock
2 Tbsp light soy sauce
2 to 3 bay leaves
450 g (1 lb) shelled sweet
   chestnuts
Salt and black pepper

Chestnuts are great cold-weather food and complement

both the flavour and texture of onions very well.

**Preparation time: 20 minutes Cooking time: 30 minutes**

Cook the onions in the oil for about 10 minutes, until soft, sweet and just starting to brown. Add the leeks, peppers and garlic and cook for a further 2 to 3 minutes.

Scatter the flour over the vegetables and stir well, then gradually add the stock. Bring slowly to the boil, stirring all the time, then add the soy sauce and bay leaves with the sweet chestnuts.

Return to the boil then cover and simmer for 30 minutes. Season to taste, adding more soy sauce if necessary, and serve with mashed potatoes.


# sweet onion *and rice bake*

*Serves 4*

6 Tbsp butter
6 sweet onions, chopped
1 cup (225 mL) quick-cooking
   long grain rice
250 mL (9 fl oz) vegetable stock
250 mL (9 fl oz) milk
Salt and black pepper
140 g (5 oz) Gruyère cheese,
   grated

In France this is traditionally an accompaniment to plain roast meat,

but I think it is a worthy main course in its own right. You need

sweet onions for the perfect flavour. If you cut down on the

butter, you will need to add extra milk with the rice.

**Preparation time: 30 minutes Cooking time: 1 hour**

Melt the butter in a large frying pan, add the onions and cook slowly for about 15 minutes, until softened and just lightly golden brown. Meanwhile, preheat the oven to 170°C/325°F/Gas Mark 3.

Stir the rice into the onions, coating it well in all the onion-flavoured juices, and cook for 2 to 3 minutes. Add the stock, milk and seasonings, then bring to the boil and simmer for 5 minutes, to par-cook the rice. The rice should still be quite moist, so add a dash more milk if necessary.

Stir in the cheese, then turn into a buttered ovenproof pan and bake, uncovered, for about an hour, until the top is browned and crisp and the rice is tender. Serve hot.

*onion and sweet chestnut casserole*

# cauliflower *and onion cheese*

*Serves 4*

1 large cauliflower, cut into
   large florets
1 large onion, cut into
   6 to 8 pieces
Salt
250 mL (9 fl oz) milk
3 Tbsp butter
3 Tbsp flour
1 tsp Dijon mustard
175 g (6 oz) Cheddar cheese,
   grated
Black pepper
2 Tbsp fresh breadcrumbs
   (optional)

I made this when my husband had an awful cold.

There's nothing like cauliflower in cheese sauce for comfort food, and onions

are said to be an effective cold remedy.

**Preparation time: 10 minutes Cooking time: 25 minutes**

Place the cauliflower and onion in a saucepan with a pinch of salt and just enough water to cover the vegetables. Bring to the boil, cover and simmer for 10 minutes.

Scoop the vegetables into an ovenproof serving dish with a slotted spoon, then reserve 250 mL (9 fl oz) of the cooking water.

Add the milk, butter and flour to the reserved water in the pan and bring slowly to the boil, stirring all the time. Cook until bubbling and thickened, then add the mustard and half the cheese. Season the sauce to taste, then pour over the vegetables in the dish.

Mix the remaining cheese with the breadcrumbs if using – this gives a crisp topping – then scatter over the dish. Brown under a hot grill before serving.

# festive red onion *spaghetti*

*Serves 4*

2 red onions, finely chopped
8 to 10 spring onions, trimmed
   and sliced on the diagonal
2 Tbsp olive oil
Pinch chilli powder
150 mL (5 fl oz) double cream
Salt and black pepper
300 g (10 oz) spaghetti, freshly
   cooked
2 tomatoes, seeded and
   chopped
A handful snipped chives

I first served this to vegetarian friends one Christmas - it was a great success.

Add grated Parmesan if you wish, but I don't think it's necessary.

**Preparation time: 10 minutes Cooking time: 10 minutes**

Cook the red onions and spring onions in the oil with the chilli powder for 2 to 3 minutes, until just softened. Add the cream, bring to the boil and simmer for 3 minutes.

Drain the spaghetti, then add it to the onion and cream sauce and mix well. Season to taste.

Stir in the chopped tomatoes and chives just before serving.

# onion *and ricotta pastries*

A really quick and easy supper dish that is surprisingly filling and very comforting!

2 large onions, finely chopped
3 Tbsp olive oil
Salt and black pepper
375 g (13 oz) packet ready-
  rolled puff pastry
Beaten egg or milk to brush
2 Tbsp yoghurt or soured cream
225 g (8 oz) ricotta cheese
1 garlic clove, minced
2 Tbsp freshly grated Parmesan
  cheese

**Preparation time: 10 minutes  Cooking time: 25 minutes**

Preheat the oven to 220°C/425°F/Gas Mark 7.

Cook the onions in the oil with salt and pepper over a medium heat for 10 to 15 minutes, until softened and lightly browned.

Meanwhile, cut the pastry into four rectangles, then make a rim of approximately 1 cm (½ in) around the edges. Brush the rim carefully with beaten egg or milk, then bake in the hot oven for 10 to 15 minutes, until golden brown.

Beat the yoghurt or soured cream into the ricotta with the garlic, Parmesan and seasoning.

Press the centres of the pastry parcels down with the back of a fork, then divide the cheese mixture among them, spreading it out gently. Top with the onion mixture, then return to the oven for 5 minutes to heat through. Serve immediately.

# sweet onion *pie*

3 large sweet onions, such as
  Vidalia, thinly sliced
4 Tbsp unsalted butter
½ tsp grated fresh nutmeg
Salt and black pepper
140 g (5 oz) plain flour
1 tsp paprika
85 g (3 oz) salted butter
2 eggs, beaten
250 mL (9 fl oz) milk
150 mL (5 fl oz) soured cream
3 Tbsp snipped fresh chives

Sweet onions usually have a white skin and a distinctive, nutty flavour.

This pie can be served as either a vegetable main dish or as an accompaniment to roast meat, or even fish. The runny filling also makes great gravy! I prefer a top-only crust, but make a double-crust pie if you prefer by doubling the pastry ingredients.

**Preparation time: 40 minutes  Cooking time: 30 minutes**

Cook the sweet onions in the butter with the nutmeg over a medium heat for about 15 minutes, until lightly golden. Season well then allow to cool slightly.

Meanwhile, preheat the oven to 200°C/400°F/Gas Mark 6. Mix the flour and paprika in a bowl and rub in the butter until the mixture resembles fine breadcrumbs. Add sufficient cold water to mix to a firm pastry dough, then turn out on to a floured surface.

Beat the eggs into the milk, soured cream and chives, then mix into the onions and turn into a suitable buttered pie dish. Roll out the pastry and use to cover the pie, using any trimmings to make decorative leaves. Make a slit in the pastry lid to allow the steam to escape, then brush with a little milk.

Place the pie dish on a baking sheet – in case the filling bubbles over – and bake in the hot oven, immediately lowering the temperature to 190°C/375°F/Gas Mark 5, for 30 minutes, or until the pastry is golden brown. Serve hot.

*sweet onion pie*

111

# sweet onion *and potato tatin*

*Serves 4 to 6*

3 large sweet onions, such as
  Vidalia, thinly sliced
3 Tbsp olive oil
1 small aubergine, sliced
6 to 7 medium potatoes, about
  800 g (1¾ lb), peeled but left
  whole
3 Tbsp butter
1 red chilli, finely chopped
Salt, black pepper and grated
  fresh nutmeg

Based on the classic upside-down apple dessert *tarte tatin*, this is a delicious layered galette of sweet onion, aubergine and potato, spiced with chilli and nutmeg.

**Preparation time: 40 minutes Cooking time: 40 minutes**

Preheat the oven to 200°C/400°F/Gas Mark 6, and place a baking sheet in the oven while it is heating up.

Cook the sliced onions in the oil with the aubergine for about 20 minutes, until all the vegetables are soft and the onions are lightly browned. Cook slowly, over a low heat.

Meanwhile, bring the potatoes to the boil in salted water, boil for 5 minutes, then drain and allow to cool slightly. Slice the potatoes thickly.

Melt half the butter in a 23 cm (9 in) deep omelette pan with an ovenproof handle, remove from the heat and scatter the chilli over the base. Season the onion mixture – adding more salt and nutmeg than pepper, then turn it into the pan over the chilli. Press flat into the pan.

Arrange the potato slices over the onions, then brush them generously with the remaining butter, melted. Season well.

Bake for 40 minutes, placing the omelette pan directly on to the hot baking sheet – this will help to caramelize the onions.

Press the potatoes down firmly with a palette knife when the tatin comes out of the oven, then loosen around the edges. Invert on to a warmed platter and serve, cut into wedges if possible, although you may resort to spoonfuls, with a salad.

# mixed bean *and onion cassoulet*

*Serves 6*

400 g (14 oz) dried mixed beans
1 red, 1 sweet and 1 large
  cooking onion, thickly sliced
3 Tbsp olive oil
Salt and black pepper
4 large thyme sprigs
400 g (14 oz) can chopped
  tomatoes
About 350 mL (12 fl oz)
  vegetable stock
280 g (10 oz) fresh
  breadcrumbs

This is real winter comfort food – serve it with fresh crusty bread and a green salad.

**Preparation time: 1½ hours, plus overnight soaking Cooking time: 1½ hours**

Soak the beans in a large bowl of water for 8 hours or overnight. Drain and rinse well in plenty of cold water.

Bring the beans to the boil in a large pan of fresh water, then cover and simmer for 1 hour. Drain and leave until required. Preheat the oven to 170°C/325°F/Gas Mark 3.

Cook the onions quickly in the oil in a flameproof casserole until just soft. Season well, then add the thyme. Pour the tomatoes over the onions, then season again.

Tip the beans over the tomatoes, pressing them down, then season well. Pour in the stock to come just below the surface of the beans.

Continue heating until the stock just comes to the boil, then cover the casserole and transfer to the oven for 1 hour.

Remove the lid and make a thick layer of breadcrumbs over the beans. Raise the oven temperature to 190°C/375°F/Gas Mark 5 and cook for a further 20 to 25 minutes, uncovered, until the breadcrumbs are browned.

# vegetable side dishes

*Perfect for entertaining or relaxed family suppers, onion side dishes add zest and colour to a meal, as well as introduce texture and bite. Onion side dishes are usually served hot, but may accompany hot or cold main dishes.*

# roasted chicory *with onion*

*Serves 4*

4 heads chicory
Lemon juice
1 red onion, finely chopped
Salt and black pepper
1–2 Tbsp olive oil

I first had chicory cooked in this way in Belgium – it has

been a favourite vegetable ever since.

**Preparation time: 10 minutes Cooking time: 40 minutes**

Preheat the oven to 200°C/400°F/Gas Mark 6.
    Cut the chicory in half lengthwise and place in a shallow roasting pan.
Add a squeeze of lemon juice. Scatter the onion on top, season lightly and drizzle
with the olive oil.
    Roast for 30 to 40 minutes, until browned and tender. Serve hot or warm.

# singapore-style *onions*

This is a vibrant way to serve onions and a delicately flavoured accompaniment to cold chicken or pork.

Preparation time: 15 minutes Cooking time: 30 minutes

Blend all the ingredients for the rempah together in a food processor, adding just enough of the water to make a rough paste.

Fry the shallots in the oil until starting to brown then add the turmeric and cook for a further 1 minute. Stir in the rempah and cook for 2 minutes.

Add the lime leaves or zest and sugar, with most of the remaining water. Bring to the boil then simmer for 10 to 15 minutes, or until the shallots are almost tender.

Blend the coconut milk with the remaining water, add to the pan and cook for a further 5 minutes. Season with salt and pepper before serving.

*Serves 4*

REMPAH (CURRY PASTE)
2 to 3 fresh red chillies
1 red onion, chopped
2 cloves garlic, chopped
2 stalks lemon grass, finely chopped
5 cm (2 in) piece fresh root ginger or galangal, peeled and chopped
25 g (1 oz) blanched almonds or macadamia nuts
250 mL (9 fl oz) water

500 g (1 lb 2 oz) shallots, peeled and left whole
1 Tbsp groundnut oil
1 tsp turmeric
6 lime leaves, shredded, or finely grated zest of 3 limes
1 Tbsp raw brown sugar
5 Tbsp coconut milk or cream
Salt and black pepper

*vegetable*

# spiced onion rice *noodles with peanut sauce*

*Serves 4 to 6*

SAUCE

2 shallots, chopped

1 red chilli, seeded and chopped

70 g (2½ oz) dry-roasted
  unsalted peanuts

5 Tbsp coconut milk or cream

250 mL (9 fl oz) water

2 Tbsp groundnut oil

1 tsp ground turmeric

1 tsp  crushed lemon grass
  paste or 1 stalk lemon grass,
  bruised and finely chopped

Salt

250 g (9 oz) medium rice
  noodles

6 spring onions, trimmed and
  finely chopped

1 Tbsp groundnut oil

115 g (4 oz) peeled prawns

½ tsp mild chilli powder

Chopped spring onions and
  crushed peanuts or prawns to
  garnish

Shredded crisp lettuce to serve

My version of Singapore street food – I've served the dish on a bed of crisp

shredded lettuce, so do sit down to eat this!

**Preparation time: 15 minutes Cooking time: 5 minutes**

Prepare the sauce. Blend the shallots, chilli, peanuts and coconut milk to a thick paste with about half the water. Heat the oil in a small pan, add the turmeric and lemon grass, and cook for a few seconds. Stir in the paste and the remaining water, then bring to the boil. Add a little salt if necessary, then keep just warm until required.

Break up the noodles in a large bowl, pour boiling water over them and leave to stand for 5 minutes.

Cook the spring onions in the oil for a few seconds, then add the prawns and chilli powder. Continue cooking until the prawns are piping hot.

Drain the noodles then add them to the onion and prawns and finally toss them in the peanut sauce. Garnish and serve on a bed of shredded lettuce.

*spiced onion rice noodles with peanut sauce*

# onion-topped *potato gratin*

*Serves 4*

1.5 kg (3–3½ lb) potatoes, or
1 kg (2¼ lb) potatoes and
500 g (1 lb 2 oz) Jerusalem
artichokes, celeriac or sweet
potato, all peeled and cut into
small pieces
2 large onions
4 Tbsp butter
1 tsp paprika
125 mL (4 fl oz) milk
Salt and black pepper
55 g (2 oz) grated Parmesan
cheese

I like to mix Jerusalem artichokes or celeriac into my potato purée.

The onion topping gilds the dish.

**Preparation time: 30 minutes Cooking time: 20-25 minutes, or 5 minutes to grill**

Preheat the oven to 220°C/425°F/Gas Mark 7, if using. Bring the potatoes and artichokes to the boil in a pan of salted water then cover and simmer for 15 to 20 minutes until tender.

Meanwhile, cook the onions slowly in the butter with the paprika until a rich golden brown.

Drain the potatoes then mash them with enough milk to make them smooth and add salt and pepper to taste. Spoon into a buttered ovenproof dish and top with the onions and Parmesan.

Bake in the hot oven for 20 to 25 minutes, until browned. Alternatively, brown quickly under a hot grill.

*vegetable*

side dishes

# fried *onions*

The classic accompaniment to all grilled meats, and a perfect addition to sandwiches and burgers, or even to liven up a salad.

*Serves 4*

4-5 Tbsp olive, sunflower or groundnut oil
4 large onions, sliced
2 bay leaves (optional)
Salt and black pepper

**Preparation time: 5 minutes Cooking time: 10–20 minutes**

Heat the oil in a large frying pan, add the onions and bay leaves and fry over a high heat for 1 to 2 minutes, stirring and tossing the onions all the time.

Lower the heat, to medium if you are in a hurry, and cook for a further 5 to 6 minutes, or to low and cook for 15 to 20 minutes. The slower the cooking, the sweeter the flavour of the onions will be. Slow cooking will also produce more tender onions.

Discard the bay leaves, season to taste and serve immediately.

# rice and *onion moulds*

This is really more of a serving suggestion than a recipe. Packing hot rice into buttered moulds makes an attractive presentation for special occasions.

I use buttered ramekins or individual pudding moulds, but old-fashioned tea cups would work just as well.

*Serves 4*

1 cup (250 mL) quick-cooking long grain rice
550 mL (19 fl oz) vegetable or chicken stock
6 to 8 spring onions, finely chopped
1-2 Tbsp chopped fresh parsley
Salt and black pepper

**Preparation time: 10 minutes Cooking time: 15 minutes**

Bring the rice to the boil in the vegetable or chicken stock. Stir once, cover, then simmer gently for 12 to 15 minutes, until all the water has been absorbed.

Generously butter 4 to 8 ramekins or moulds. Stir the onions into the rice with the chopped parsley and season well. Pack the mixture into the prepared moulds and press down firmly.

Unmould carefully on to warmed serving plates and use immediately.

# onions braised *in balsamic vinegar*

*Serves 4*

16 to 20 silverskin onions or
  shallots
1 red chilli, seeded and sliced
2 sun-dried tomatoes, finely
  sliced
Salt and black pepper
5 Tbsp balsamic vinegar
2 Tbsp olive oil

A great accompaniment to rich creamy pasta dishes and

an interesting alternative to salad side dishes.

**Preparation time: 10 minutes Cooking time: 15 minutes**

Preheat the oven to 190°C/375°F/Gas Mark 5. Bring the onions to the boil in a pan of salted water and simmer for 5 minutes. Drain.

Butter a small ovenproof pan that will take the onions in one layer and place the chilli and tomatoes in the base. Arrange the onions on top and season generously, then pour over the vinegar and oil.

Braise, uncovered, in the oven for 15 minutes, or until the onions are tender. Baste with the vinegar twice during cooking. Serve warm.

# shallots braised *with sour cherries*

*Serves 4*

2 Tbsp groundnut oil
8 banana shallots or 16 large
  button shallots
2 lime leaves, shredded, or
  finely grated zest of 1 lime
50 g (1¾ oz) sour cherries
Salt and black pepper
250 mL (9 fl oz) vegetable stock
1 Tbsp sugar

Sour cherries add a note of sweetness to the onions,

cooked slowly to draw out their full flavour.

**Preparation time: 20 minutes Cooking time: 30 minutes**

Preheat the oven to 190°C/75°F/Gas Mark 5.

Heat the oil in a medium frying pan, add the shallots and cook slowly for 10 to 12 minutes, until well browned but just starting to soften. This method of cooking brings out their natural sweetness.

Transfer the shallots to a small casserole dish that will take them in a single layer. Bury the lime leaves among them, or sprinkle over the lime zest, together with the cherries, season well and pour in the stock. Sprinkle with sugar.

Cover the casserole, then place it in the hot oven. Cook for 25 to 30 minutes, until the shallots are tender. Season to taste then serve the shallots and cherries with the juices spooned over.

# spiced fried *onions with rice*

A great dish to serve with rich meats in creamy sauces,

or with cold leftovers from a roast.

**Serves 4**

**Preparation time: 10 minutes Cooking time: 20 minutes**

Heat the oil in a large pan, then add the onions, spices and bay leaves and cook for 4 to 5 minutes.

Stir in the rice and toss in the juices, add the stock and salt and bring to the boil. Stir, then cover and simmer for 12 to 15 minutes. Season to taste before serving.

3 Tbsp groundnut or
  sunflower oil
2 large onions, sliced
1 Tbsp onion seeds
1 large cinnamon stick, broken
2 pieces star anise
6 black peppercorns
2 bay leaves
200 g (7 oz) quick-cooking
  long grain rice
450 mL (16 fl oz) vegetable or
  chicken stock
Salt

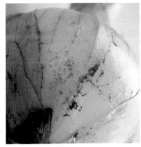

# thai *spiced onions*

*Serves 4*

2 Tbsp groundnut oil

1 Tbsp coriander seeds, lightly
  crushed

1 stalk lemon grass, bruised
  and finely chopped

1 green and 1 red chilli, seeded
  and finely chopped

2 large onions, thickly sliced

1 red onion, cut into 8
  segments

10 to 12 spring onions, cut into
  5 cm (2 in) pieces, finely
  sliced lengthways

2 Tbsp fish sauce

Lime juice and salt to taste

Shredded coconut and fresh
  coriander to garnish

These onions are only lightly cooked, to retain flavour and colour. This makes

an excellent side dish with grilled fish.

Preparation time: 10 minutes Cooking time: 5 minutes

Heat the oil in a large frying pan or wok, then add the coriander seeds, lemon grass and chillies. Fry quickly for 1 to 2 minutes.

Stir the sliced onions and the red onion into the frying pan and stir-fry quickly for approximately 2 to 3 minutes.

Add the spring onions and toss them in the juices. Heat for just a few seconds, then stir in the fish sauce. Add lime juice and salt to taste.

Serve the onions garnished with coconut and fresh coriander.

# two-bean *mash with onions*

*Serves 4 to 6*

150 g (5½ oz) dried lima beans

150 g (5½ oz) dried cannellini
  beans

2 large onions, finely sliced

2 Tbsp olive oil

1–2 Tbsp chopped fresh
  rosemary

Salt and black pepper

A great change from plain mashed potatoes,

and especially good with roast lamb.

Preparation time: 10 minutes, plus overnight soaking Cooking time: 1¼ hours

Soak the beans together in cold water for 8 hours or overnight, then drain and rinse them thoroughly.

Bring the beans to the boil in a pan of salted water with half the onions, then cover and simmer for 1 hour, or until tender.

Cook the remaining onion in the oil with the rosemary until golden brown.

Drain the beans – I usually reserve the cooking liquid to use in soups. Mash lightly – you don't want a completely uniform texture – then stir in the fried onions. Season well before serving.

# glazed *roasted onions*

This is a marvellous onion antipasto, which makes a welcome change from vegetables in oil. The onions may also be served with cold cuts.

*Serves 4*

4 sweet white onions, such as
 Vidalia
Salt and black pepper
3 Tbsp orange juice
1 Tbsp balsamic vinegar
2 Tbsp olive oil

**Preparation time: 10 minutes Cooking time: 30 minutes**

Preheat the oven to 220°C/425°F/Gas Mark 7.

Peel the onions, leaving the root intact, then cut them through in half – the root will hold them together during cooking.

Place the onions, cut side down, in a small ovenproof pan just big enough to take them all. Season lightly, then spoon the remaining ingredients over the onions. Roast in the hot oven for about 25 to 30 minutes, basting occasionally.

Serve the onions warm or cold.

# baked shallots *with garlic breadcrumbs*

*Serves 4*

2 Tbsp olive oil

16 shallots, about 500 g (1 lb)

Salt and black pepper

Pinch of ground mace

150 mL (5 fl oz) vegetable
  stock

4 Tbsp butter

85 g (3 oz) fresh white
  breadcrumbs

1 garlic clove, minced

Pinch of paprika

The subtle flavour of garlic in the breadcrumb topping is the ideal way to finish this simple dish.

**Preparation time: 20 minutes Cooking time: 35-40 minutes**

Preheat the oven to 190°C/375°F/Gas Mark 5. Heat the oil in a small heatproof casserole, then add the shallots and cook them quickly until browned all over.

Season the shallots with salt, pepper and mace, then pour the stock into the pan. Bring to the boil, cover with a lid or foil and place in the hot oven for 20 minutes, until the shallots are tender.

Remove the casserole lid and boil away any surplus stock – it should be well reduced to a thickish syrup.

Melt the butter, add the breadcrumbs and garlic and toss them together, adding a little salt, pepper and paprika for colour. Spoon the crumbs over the shallots, then return them to the oven for 10 to 15 minutes, until browned. Serve hot.

# champ

A traditional Irish dish which combines potatoes and spring onions. I could

eat it just as it is, although it is more usual to serve it as an accompaniment.

**Preparation time: 10 minutes Cooking time: 25 minutes**

Peel the potatoes and cut them into small pieces. Bring to the boil in a pan of salted water, then cover and simmer for 15 to 20 minutes, until tender.

Meanwhile, simmer the spring onions gently in the milk for 2 to 3 minutes.

Drain the potatoes, then return them to the pan and place them over a low heat for a minute or so, to allow any excess water to evaporate.

Add the milk and onions and pound or beat the potatoes to a soft, fluffy mash. Add plenty of salt and pepper as you go. Mound the champ in a large bowl. Make a little hollow for the butter and allow it to melt into the potatoes before serving.

*Serves 4*

800 g (1³/₄ lb) potatoes
1 bunch spring onions, about 8 to
  10, trimmed and finely sliced
150 mL (5 fl oz) milk
Salt and black pepper
115 g (4 oz) butter

# onion, potato *and bacon rösti*

*Serves 4 to 6*

6 potatoes, unpeeled, about
  800 g (1¾ lb)
6 bacon rashers
1 large red onion
Salt, black pepper and grated
  fresh nutmeg
2 Tbsp butter
2 Tbsp sunflower oil

I have never been successful at rösti – until now! I think chilling the

par-cooked potatoes before grating them has been the answer.

**Preparation time: 30 minutes, plus 1-2 hours chilling time Cooking time: 10 minutes**

Bring a pan of salted water to the boil, add the potatoes, cover and allow to boil for 15 minutes. Drain, then rinse thoroughly under cold water. Chill the potatoes for at least 1 hour in the fridge – 2 to 3 hours is better.

Chop the bacon finely in the food processor, then fry it until well browned in a large non-stick frying pan.

Meanwhile, chop the onion in the food processor, then fit the coarse grating attachment. Scrape the skins off the chilled potatoes then grate them into the onion. Turn into a bowl and mix the crisp bacon into the potatoes and onion with the seasonings. Shape into 8 flat, round patties.

Heat the butter with the oil in the frying pan, then add the rösti mixture. Press down firmly, then cook over a moderately high heat for 3 to 4 minutes on each side. Press the rösti down firmly again when you turn them. Cook the röstis in 2 batches if necessary, and serve piping hot.

# breads & bakes

*There are a whole range of breads which can be baked with onions for extra flavour – chopped fresh vegetables or dried soup mixes will both add an extra taste dimension to your baking, and sliced onions sprinkled over a loaf make a most attractive garnish.*

# pissaladière

Serves 6 to 8

550 g (1¼ lb) onions, sliced
3 Tbsp olive oil
4 to 5 large thyme sprigs
Salt and black pepper
2 bay leaves
225 g (8 oz) white bread flour
½ tsp salt
1 tsp instant dry yeast
2 Tbsp olive oil
55 g (2 oz) can anchovy fillets
8 to 10 black or green olives,
  halved

One of my very favourite foods – a pure onion pizza! It's great on its own, but it is also wonderful served in slices with roast beef and vegetables, as an alternative to potatoes. I think it is much better if you stew the onions first to get the juices for making the dough – it takes hours, but it is worth it.

**Preparation time: 3½ hours Cooking time: 25–30 minutes**

Cook the onions in the oil in a large frying pan for 4 to 5 minutes over a high heat. Stir in the thyme, plenty of salt and pepper and the bay leaves, then cover the frying pan and allow to stew slowly for up to 2 hours.

Turn the onions into a sieve over a jug and allow all the juices to drain through.

Mix the flour, salt and yeast together in a bowl, then add the olive oil and the onion juices – you should have about 150 mL (5 fl oz). Mix to a soft, manageable dough then knead thoroughly on a floured surface.

Roll out the dough and press it in a thin layer into the base of a pan about 40 x 25 cm (16 x 10 in) – it may not reach quite to the corners but will spread out as it rises. Cover with a damp cloth or clear film and leave in a warm place for about 1 hour, until almost doubled in size.

Preheat the oven to 220°C/425°F/Gas Mark 7. Remove the bay leaves and thyme, then spread the onions over the risen dough. Arrange the anchovy fillets and olives over the onions and drizzle with the oil from the anchovies.

Bake in the preheated oven for 25 to 30 minutes, until the bread base and the onions are browned. Serve warm, cut into fingers.

*pissaladière*

129

# ploughman's *bread*

*Makes 1 large loaf*

225 g (8 oz) white bread flour

225 g (8 oz) wholemeal bread
flour

½ tsp salt

1 tsp instant dry yeast

25 g (1 oz) packet dried onion
soup mix

2 Tbsp olive oil

115 g (4 oz) Cheddar cheese,
grated

150 mL (5 fl oz) beer

About 150 mL (5 fl oz) warm
water

1 Tbsp chopped onion to
garnish

A traditional blend of bread, cheese, onions and beer – in a loaf! This is almost a meal in itself, but, thickly spread with butter it is delicious with coleslaw and green salad leaves.

**Preparation time: 1½ hours Cooking time: 40 minutes**

Mix the flours, salt and yeast in a large bowl, then stir in the soup mix, the olive oil and most of the cheese. Make a well in the centre and add the beer, then gradually add the water, mixing to a manageable dough.

Turn out on to a floured work surface and knead thoroughly for about 10 minutes, until the dough is smooth and quite elastic. Shape into a loaf and place in a 900 g (2 lb) loaf pan, pressing the dough into the corners of the pan. Cover with a damp cloth or clear film and allow to rise in a warm place for about 1¼ hours, until doubled in size.

Preheat the oven to 220°C/425°F/Gas Mark 7. Mix the remaining cheese with the chopped onion and sprinkle over the loaf. Bake in the hot oven for 35 to 40 minutes. Remove the loaf from the pan. Return the loaf to the oven for 5 minutes, if necessary, to crisp the base – it should sound hollow when tapped.

Cool the loaf on a wire rack. Serve sliced, with cheese and salad.

# goat's cheese *and cinnamon onion rolls*

These rolls, bursting with unusual flavours, are perfect to serve with soup at a dinner party.

**Preparation time: 1³/₄ hours Cooking time: 30 minutes**

Cook the onions with the cinnamon in 2 tablespoons (25 mL) of the oil in a large frying pan for 10 to 15 minutes, until the onions are softened and lightly browned. Season well, then allow to cool.

Mix the flour with the salt and yeast, add the remaining oil, then mix to a soft but manageable dough with the water – adjust the quantity of water as necessary.

Turn the dough on to a lightly floured surface and knead thoroughly for about 10 minutes, until smooth and elastic, then divide into 8 pieces.

Mix the goat's cheese with the cooled onions.

Flatten each piece of dough out into a circle and divide the onion and cheese filling among the pieces. Brush the edges of the dough with water, then gather it around the filling. Turn over and roll lightly to a circle about 7.5 cm (3 in) across. Place on oiled baking sheets, cover with damp cloths or clear film and leave in a warm place to rise for about 1¹/₄ hours until roughly doubled in size.

Preheat the oven to 180°C/350°F/Gas Mark 4. Bake the rolls for about 30 minutes until lightly golden. Cool slightly before serving.

*Makes 8 large rolls*

2 large onions, thinly sliced
¹/₂ tsp ground cinnamon
5 Tbsp olive oil
Salt and black pepper
500 g (1 lb) white bread flour
1 tsp salt
2 tsp instant dry yeast
About 250 mL (9 fl oz) warm water
225 g (8 oz) soft goat's cheese, crumbled

# onion *and pecan nut bread*

*Makes 1 large loaf*

225 g (8 oz) white bread flour

225 g (8 oz) wholemeal bread
flour

1 tsp salt

1 tsp instant dry yeast

115 g (4 oz) pecan nut pieces,
finely chopped

1 medium onion, grated

1 Tbsp clear honey

2 Tbsp olive oil

250 mL (9 fl oz) warm milk, or
milk and water mixed

This loaf has a light texture and is allowed to rise twice, even when made

with fast-acting yeast. It is very much a French-style loaf.

**Preparation time: about 2 hours Cooking time: 30 minutes**

Mix together the flours, salt and yeast in a large bowl, then stir in the pecan nuts and
grated onion.

Beat the honey with the olive oil, then pour it into the flour. Gradually add the
milk, mixing to a firm but manageable dough. Turn on to a floured surface and knead
thoroughly until smooth – because of the wholemeal flour this dough will not be as
elastic as others. Return to the bowl, cover with a damp cloth or clear film and leave
in a warm place for at least 1 hour, until doubled in size.

Punch down the dough and then knead lightly again. Shape into a round loaf and
place on an oiled baking sheet. Cover again and leave for 30 minutes.

Preheat the oven to 220°C/425°F/Gas Mark 7. Sprinkle the loaf with a little flour,
then bake in the hot oven for about 30 minutes – the base of the loaf will sound
hollow when tapped when the loaf is done. Cool on a wire rack before serving.

# scottish onion *baps*

These home-made floury milk rolls are wonderful, with a soft crust. It's the

perfect roll to hold burgers or salad.

**Makes 8**

500 g (1 lb) white bread flour

1 tsp salt

1 tsp instant dry yeast

2 Tbsp lard

1 medium onion, very finely chopped

2 spring onions, very finely chopped

250 mL (9 fl oz) warm milk and water mixed

**Preparation time: 1¼ hours Cooking time: 15–20 minutes**

Mix together the flour, salt and yeast, then cut in the lard. Stir in the chopped onions. Mix to a soft, manageable dough with the milk and water, adding a little more warm liquid if necessary.

Turn the dough on to a lightly floured surface and knead thoroughly for about 10 minutes, until smooth and elastic. Divide the dough into 8 and roll out into buns about 1 cm (½ in) thick, placing them on to floured baking sheets.

Cover the baps with damp dish towels or clear film and allow to rise in a warm place for about 1 hour until roughly doubled in size.

Preheat the oven to 200°C/400°F/Gas Mark 6. Dredge the baps with a little extra flour, then bake them in the hot oven for 15 to 20 minutes, until lightly golden. Cool on a wire rack before splitting and serving.

# onion *seed rolls*

These are great with cheese, cold meat and pickles. The onion seeds provide

both flavour and a delicious, crunchy texture.

**Makes 12**

500 g (1 lb) white bread flour

1 tsp salt

1 tsp (5 mL) easy-blend dry yeast

25 g (1 oz) packet onion soup mix

1 Tbsp black onion seeds, lightly crushed

3 Tbsp olive oil

250 mL (9 fl oz) warm water

Flour to dredge

**Preparation time: 1 hour 20 minutes Cooking time: 25 minutes**

Mix the flour, salt and yeast together in a bowl, then stir in the soup mix and the onion seeds. Make a well in the centre and add the olive oil with enough warm water to mix to a soft but manageable dough.

Turn out on to a floured work surface and knead thoroughly until smooth and elastic – about 10 minutes. Divide into 12, shape into rolls, then place them on floured baking sheets. Cover with damp cloths or clear film and leave to rise in a warm place for about 1 hour, until roughly doubled in size.

Preheat the oven to 220°C/425°F/Gas Mark 7. Dust the rolls lightly with more flour, then bake them in the hot oven for 20 to 25 minutes, until lightly golden. Allow to cool on a wire rack before serving.

# roast red onion and *thyme bread*

*Makes 1 large loaf*

2 red onions, halved

²/₃ cup (150 mL) extra virgin
   olive oil

Salt and black pepper

500 g (1 lb) white bread flour

2 tsp instant dry yeast

250 mL (9 fl oz) warm water

1 Tbsp salt

2 Tbsp fresh thyme leaves

Olive oil and coarse sea salt to
   finish

Allowing the yeast mixture to stand for an hour before mixing develops a slightly sour, authentic Italian bread flavour.

**Preparation time: 3 hours Cooking time: 40 minutes**

Preheat the oven to 220°C/425°F/Gas Mark 7. Place the onions in a small pan, drizzle with 1 tablespoon of the olive oil and season well with salt and pepper. Roast in the hot oven for 45 minutes, allow to cool slightly and chop finely. Turn the oven off.

Meanwhile, measure 5 tablespoons of flour into a large mixing bowl and combine it with the yeast and half the warm water – there is no need to mix to a smooth paste. Cover the bowl with clear film or a damp cloth and leave for 1 hour.

Stir in the oil, salt and thyme, then add the chopped onion and the remaining flour. Mix to a soft manageable dough with the remaining water, adding it gradually, with a little extra if necessary.

Turn the dough on to a lightly floured surface and knead thoroughly for about 10 minutes, until smooth and no longer sticky. Alternatively, knead in a food mixer fitted with a dough hook.

Shape the dough then press it into an oiled pan about 17.5 x 27.5 cm (7 x 11 in). Cover as before and leave in a warm place to rise for 1¹/₂ hours, until roughly doubled in size – this takes longer than usual because of the amount of oil in the dough.

Reheat the oven to 220°C/425°F/Gas Mark 7. Slash the surface of the loaf several times with a sharp knife, drizzle with extra oil then sprinkle with coarse salt.

Bake for 35 to 40 minutes until golden. The cooked loaf should leave the pan easily and be well browned on the base (it's too rich to sound really hollow when tapped). Cool for at least 10 minutes before eating.

# onion and *rosemary focaccia*

This is a classic Italian loaf, made with olive oil and here topped with sliced onion rings and fresh rosemary.

*Makes 1 large loaf*

500 g (1 lb) white bread flour
1 tsp salt
1 tsp instant dry yeast
6 Tbsp olive oil
About 250 mL (9 fl oz) warm water
2 large onions, sliced into thin rings
1-2 Tbsp chopped fresh rosemary
Coarse sea salt

**Preparation time: 1³/₄ hours Cooking time: 30 minutes**

Mix the flour, salt and yeast together in a bowl, make a well in the centre and add the oil and enough water to make a manageable dough.

Turn on to a lightly floured surface and knead the dough thoroughly for about 10 minutes, until smooth and elastic. Roll out the dough then press into an oiled baking pan about 40 x 25 cm (16 x 10 in) – press the dough right up into the corners. Cover with a damp cloth or clear film and leave in a warm place for 1 to 1¹/₂ hours, until well risen and doubled in size.

Meanwhile, soak the onion rings in cold water to soften them.

Preheat the oven to 220°C/425°F/Gas Mark 7. Drain the onion rings and arrange them on the loaf, then sprinkle with the rosemary and salt.

Bake in the preheated oven for 25 to 30 minutes, until the loaf is a pale golden brown and the onions are soft. Allow to cool on a wire rack before eating.

# spinach and *onion cornbread*

*Makes 1 large loaf*

125 g (4½ oz) fine yellow
   cornmeal
140 g (5 oz) plain flour
2 tsp baking powder
Pinch of salt
2 red onions, very finely
   chopped
125 g (4½ oz) very finely
   chopped spinach
Black pepper
2 large eggs, separated
150 mL (9 fl oz) milk
150 mL (9 fl oz) double cream

An extremely versatile cornbread that is not too sweet.

Quick to mix and bake, this bread may be served hot as an alternative to

potatoes or rice, or cold with cheese or cold meats.

**Preparation time: 25 minutes Cooking time: 50 minutes**

Preheat the oven to 190°C/375°F/Gas Mark 5, and lightly butter a deep 20–23 cm (9 in) cake pan.

Mix the cornmeal, flour, baking powder and salt together, then stir in the onions and chopped spinach with plenty of black pepper.

Beat the egg yolks with the milk and cream, then pour into the bowl and stir to combine thoroughly. Whisk the egg whites until stiff, then fold them evenly into the onion and spinach mixture.

Turn the cornbread into the prepared pan and bake in the preheated oven for about 45 minutes, until lightly browned and set.

Cool the bread in the pan for about 10 minutes before cutting. Serve warm with cheese, or instead of potatoes with a roast.

# quick onion and *tomato bread*

*Makes 1 loaf*

225 g (8 oz) fine wholemeal
   flour
1 tsp baking powder
½ tsp salt
2 Tbsp chopped fresh parsley
1 red onion, grated
2 tomatoes, skinned, seeded
   and chopped
2 sun-dried tomatoes, finely
   shredded
2 Tbsp olive oil
1 large egg, beaten
About 125 mL (4 fl oz) milk

More of a scone loaf than a bread, but an excellent

bake to serve with soup or a winter salad.

**Preparation time: 15 minutes Cooking time: 40 minutes**

Preheat the oven to 190°C/375°F/Gas Mark 5, and lightly oil a 900 g (2 lb) loaf pan.

Mix together the dry ingredients with the parsley, then stir in the onion and tomatoes. Add the oil and egg, then enough milk to form a soft dough, but not too wet.

Tip the mixture into the prepared pan and press down lightly. Don't bother to smooth the top – it looks better a bit rough! Bake the bread in the preheated oven for about 40 minutes, until golden brown.

Carefully turn the loaf out of the pan on to a wire rack and cool for at least 10 minutes before cutting.

# spring onion soda *bread*

This is a marvellous bread to serve with various cheeses at an informal meal.

**Preparation time: 15 minutes Cooking time: 30 minutes**

Preheat the oven to 220°C/425°F/Gas Mark 7 and lightly butter a baking sheet.

Mix the flours in a large bowl with the salt and bicarbonate of soda, then rub in the butter until the mixture resembles breadcrumbs. Stir in the spring onions and the buttermilk or yoghurt mixture.

Mix quickly and lightly to a slightly soft but manageable dough – use a spatula and mix with quick strokes. The worst thing you can do to soda bread is overmix it. Add a little extra milk if necessary.

Knead the dough very lightly – just enough to make it into a large round, about 4 cm (1½ in) thick. Place on the baking sheet and mark into 8 sections.

Bake in the hot oven for 30 minutes, until well browned. Allow to cool on a wire rack and serve buttered.

*Makes 1 large loaf*

350 g (12 oz) wholemeal flour
115 g (4 oz) plain flour
1 tsp salt
1 tsp bicarbonate of soda
4 Tbsp butter
6 spring onions, trimmed and
  finely chopped
250 mL (9 fl oz) buttermilk or
  yoghurt and milk mixed

# poppy seed and *red onion focaccia*

*Makes 1 loaf*

500 g (1 lb) white bread flour

1 tsp salt

5 Tbsp onion seeds

1 tsp instant dry yeast

2 red onions, grated or very
finely chopped

3 Tbsp olive oil

250 mL (9 fl oz) warm water

Olive oil to finish

A seeded, soft bread made with olive oil, with a tang of onion.

Great for lazy Saturday lunches.

**Preparation time: 1³/₄ hours Cooking time: 30-35 minutes**

Mix the flour, salt, onion seeds and yeast in a large bowl, then stir in the onions. Make a well in the centre, add the olive oil then add most of the water. Mix to a soft manageable dough, adding more water if necessary.

Turn on to a lightly floured surface, then knead thoroughly until the dough is smooth, elastic and no longer sticky. Press into a pan about 20 x 30 cm (8 x 12 in), then cover with a damp cloth or clear film and leave in a warm place for 1 to 1¹/₂ hours, until well risen and doubled in size.

Preheat the oven to 220°C/425°F/Gas Mark 7. Brush the risen dough with oil, then bake in the hot oven for 30 to 35 minutes, or until the bread is golden and the base sounds hollow when tapped. Cool on a wire rack before cutting into squares to serve.

*poppy seed and red onion focaccia*

# red pesto and *red onion stick*

*Makes 1 loaf*

1 large red onion, cut into fine
   rings
280 g (10 oz) white bread flour
½ tsp salt
1 tsp instant dry yeast
1 Tbsp olive oil
About 175 mL (6 fl oz) warm
   water
3 Tbsp red or standard green
   basil pesto

An unusual bread, great to serve with soup.

The dough is spread with pesto and onions and then rolled so that it

is swirled with colour when baked and sliced.

**Preparation time: 1½ hours Cooking time: 30 minutes**

Soak the onion rings in cold water until required to soften them.

Mix the flour, salt and yeast in a bowl, then add the olive oil and enough warm water to make a fairly firm, manageable dough. Turn on to a floured surface and knead thoroughly until smooth and elastic.

Roll and gently pull the dough into a rough rectangle shape, approximately 20 x 25 cm (8 x 10 in), then spread it with the pesto sauce.

Drain the onions, shake them dry, then sprinkle them over the pesto. Roll the dough up from one of the long sides, moisten the edge and seal it together firmly. Place the stick on a baking sheet with the seam underneath. Cover with a damp cloth or clear film and leave in a warm place for at least an hour, until doubled in size.

Preheat the oven to 200°C/400°F/Gas Mark 6. Slash the dough diagonally about 6 or 8 times, then bake the stick in the hot oven for 30 minutes, until golden brown. Cool on a wire rack then slice or tear into chunks.

# cheese and onion *malted grain rolls*

*Makes 12*

350 g (12 oz) malted grain
   flour
225 g (8 oz) strong white bread
   flour
1 tsp salt
2 tsp instant dry yeast
2 red onions, peeled and grated
3 Tbsp olive oil
250 mL (9 fl oz) warm milk
About 150 mL (5 fl oz) warm
   water
115 g (4 oz) Cheddar cheese,
   grated

Malted grain flour makes a delicious, nut-flavoured bread.

I've added some onions and cheese for an extra treat.

**Preparation time: 1½ hours Cooking time: 20-25 minutes**

Mix the flours, salt and yeast together in a large bowl, then mix in the grated onion. Make a well in the centre, and add the oil and milk and enough warm water to make a soft but manageable dough.

Turn out on to a lightly floured surface and knead the dough thoroughly until smooth and elastic and no longer sticky.

Divide into 12 and shape into rolls, placing them quite close together on two baking sheets. Cover with damp cloths or clear film and allow to rise in a warm place for about 1 hour, until doubled in size.

Preheat the oven to 220°C/425°F/Gas Mark 7. Sprinkle the rolls with the cheese, then bake in the hot oven for about 20 minutes, until golden and crusty.

Cool on a wire rack.

# onion and *buttermilk rye bread*

I first tasted bread similar to this in Poland. It is a dense bread with a deliciously sharp flavour. It contains no white flour, so don't expect it to rise too much.

*Makes 2 loaves*

500 g (1 lb) light rye flour, sieved
225 g (8 oz) wholemeal flour
1 tsp salt
1 tsp grated nutmeg
1½ tsp instant dry yeast
1 large onion, grated
3 Tbsp olive oil
300 mL (10 fl oz) buttermilk
Milk, rye flour and onion seeds to decorate

**Preparation time: 2 hours Cooking time: 40 minutes**

Mix together the flours, salt, nutmeg and yeast in a large bowl, then stir in the onion. Make a well in the centre and add the oil and buttermilk. Mix to a soft but manageable dough, adding a little milk or water if necessary.

Turn on to a lightly floured surface and knead thoroughly for about 10 minutes – the dough will become smooth but not very elastic. Divide into 2 and shape into rounds about 20 cm (8 in) in diameter. Place on oiled baking sheets, then cover with damp dish towels or clear film and allow to rise for about an hour or until roughly doubled in size.

Preheat the oven to 220°C/425°F/Gas Mark 7. Score each loaf into 8 before baking, then brush with milk and sprinkle with flour and onion seeds. Bake in the hot oven for 30 to 35 minutes, until the bases sound hollow when tapped. Cool on a wire rack before cutting and serving in wedges.

# onion *pretzels*

*Makes 18*

1 Tbsp butter

250 mL (9 fl oz) milk

100 mL (3½ fl oz) water

500 g (1 lb) white bread flour

1 tsp salt

1 tsp instant dry yeast

1 tsp onion seeds

1 egg, beaten

Coarse salt and onion seeds to
  decorate

A really fun bread to create and shape, and one that

children will enjoy helping to make.

**Preparation time: 2 hours Cooking time: 20 minutes**

Warm the butter in the milk and water until just melted.

Mix the flour, salt, yeast and onion seeds in a large bowl, then gradually add the liquid, mixing to a slightly sticky dough. Knead thoroughly in the bowl, until the mixture leaves the sides cleanly. Leave the dough in the bowl, cover with a damp cloth or clear film and leave in a warm place for about an hour, until doubled in size.

Preheat the oven to 240°C/475°F/Gas Mark 9. Knead the dough gently on a lightly floured surface, then divide it into 18 pieces. Roll each one into a thin pencil-shaped log about 30 cm (12 in) long. Lay the roll in front of you in the shape of a horseshoe, then fold the ends up and across, pressing them into the traditional pretzel shape. Arrange on baking sheets and leave for 10 minutes.

Brush the pretzels with egg, then sprinkle with coarse salt and onion seeds. Place in the hot oven, immediately lower the temperature to 200°C/400°F/Gas Mark 6 and bake for 20 minutes, until golden brown.

Cool on a wire rack and serve on their own or with dips.

# index

## Useful Addresses

Suttons
Woodview Road
Paignton
Devon TQ4 7NG
Tel: 01803 696300
Fax: 01803 696345
Range of onion seeds and sets, bulb onions, salad onions, pickling onions and Japanese onions.

Mr Fothergill's Seeds
Gazeley Road
Kentford
Newmarket
Suffolk
CB8 7QB
Tel: 01638 552512
Fax: 01638 750468
Range of onion sets and seeds, including shallots and garlic. Some sets exclusive to Fothergill's e.g. British Bulldog onion. Mail order catalogue available.

E. W. King & Co. Ltd.
Monks Farm
Kelvedon
Colchester
Essex
CO5 9PG
Tel: 01376 570000
Fax: 01376 571189
Extensive range of onion seeds and sets. Seed varieties include Long Red Florence, Crimson

Forest, Purplette, Red Baron and Red Brunswick. Catalogue available.
Future Foods
PO Box 1564
Wedmore
Somerset
BS28 4DP
Tel/Fax: 01934 713623
E-mail: enquiry@seeds.cix.co.uk
http://www.futurefoods.com
Supplies muliplier onions of various kinds (potato onions, shallots etc.) and also Tree Onions, Babbington's Leeks and many other alliums, including Rocambole. Twice-yearly catalogue available.

E. Marshall & Co. Ltd.
Wisbech
Cambridgeshire
PE13 2RF
Tel: 01945 583407
Fax: 01945 588235
Several varieties of onion seeds and sets including exclusive varieties: Marshall's Showmaster, Marshall's Giant Fen Globe. Catalogue available.

Simpsons Seeds
27 Meadowbrook
Old Oxted
Surrey
RH8 9LT
Tel/Fax: 01883 715242

Onion seeds: North Holland Blood-Red Red Mate, spring onions and the legendary American Walla Walla Sweets. Catalogue available.
Organic Gardening Catalogue
Riverdene Business Park
Molsey Road
Hersham
Surrey
KT12 4RG
Tel: 01932 253666

Edwin Tucker & Sons Ltd.
Brewery Meadow
Stonepark
Ashburton
Newton Abbot
Devon
TQ13 7DG
Tel: 01364 652403
Over 12 types of onion seeds and 7 different onion sets including autumn-planting Radar. Will obtain unusual varieties to order. Catalogue available.